RESTRUCTURING FOR INNOVATION

YO -BUT -617

PERSPECTIVES ON ECONOMIC CHANGE

Series Editors

Peter Dicken
University of Manchester

Meric Gertler
University of Toronto

TRADING INDUSTRIES, TRADING REGIONS:
INTERNATIONAL TRADE, AMERICAN INDUSTRY,
AND REGIONAL ECONOMIC DEVELOPMENT
Helzi Noponen, Julie Graham, and Ann R. Markusen, Editors

RESTRUCTURING FOR INNOVATION:
THE REMAKING OF THE U.S.
SEMICONDUCTOR INDUSTRY
David P. Angel

RESTRUCTURING FOR INNOVATION

The Remaking of the
U.S. Semiconductor Industry

DAVID P. ANGEL

THE GUILFORD PRESS
New York London

© 1994 The Guilford Press
A Division of Guilford Publications, Inc.
72 Spring Street, New York, NY 10012

Marketed and distributed outside North America by Longman Group UK Limited

Printed in the United States of America

This book is printed on acid-free paper.

Last digit is print number: 9 8 7 6 5 4 3 2 1

Library of Congress Cataloging-in-Publication Data

Angel, David P.
    Restructuring for innovation : the remaking of the U.S.
semiconductor industry / David P. Angel.
        p.   cm. — (Perspectives on economic change)
    Includes bibliographical references and index.
    ISBN 0-89862-297-2
    1. Semiconductor industry—United States. I. Title. II. Series.
HD9696.S43U443   1994
338.4'762138152'0973—dc20   93-40423
                                                                CIP

Acknowledgments

Research for this book was supported in part by the National Science Foundation under grant numbers SES-8701108 and SES-9109650. As with any extended project, this book would not have been possible without the support and encouragement provided by many friends and colleagues. Initial work was completed under the guidance of Professor Allen Scott, Department of Geography, UCLA. The faculty, students, and staff of the Graduate School of Geography, Clark University, created an ideal academic environment within which to bring the work to fruition. Professor Peter Dicken provided insightful comments on an earlier draft of the manuscript. Finally, I would like to thank members of the semiconductor industry who on countless occasions provided information and took the time to answer my questions with care and attention. The book is dedicated to my wife, Jocelyne.

Contents

CHAPTER 1

Introduction

The 1980s were a period of painful and far-reaching adjustment for the U.S. semiconductor industry. After three decades of technological and commercial domination, U.S. semiconductor firms in the 1980s generally lost market share and technological leadership to Japan. By 1986 Japan had surpassed the United States as the largest producer of semiconductors in the world, and Japanese firms were assuming an increasingly dominant position in key enabling technologies, such as lithography and factory automation. In 1989 Japan ran a trade surplus in semiconductors with the United States of more than $1.5 billion (Integrated Circuit Engineering Corporation [ICE] 1992). With Japanese producers outspending international competitors in R&D and capital equipment, industry observers warned of a possible domino effect in which U.S. firms would be driven out of profitable segments of the semiconductor industry and other allied high technology sectors of production, such as computers and communication systems (National Advisory Committee on Semiconductors [NACS] 1989).

How did this rapid shift in market position come about? One influential line of analysis places primary emphasis on unfair trade practices and government subsidies in Japan (Prestowitz 1988). More recently, however, researchers have begun to question the international competitiveness and durability of semiconductor manufacturing practices in the United States (Ferguson 1988; Florida and Kenney 1989, 1990b). With or without government subsidies, these authors argue, the fabled entrepreneurs and start-up firms of Silicon Valley are no match for the large firm Keiretsu of Japan or the Chaebol of South

Korea. Once celebrated for their innovative dynamism and growth potential, start-up semiconductor firms in Silicon Valley are now often blamed for the industrial fragmentation and resource dissipation that are (or so it is claimed) undermining the competitiveness of the United States in high-technology sectors of production. Florida and Kenney (1990a), among others, advocate the redirection of resources away from Silicon Valley start-up firms and toward large vertically integrated electronics conglomerates. At the same time, many analysts call for government intervention to help underwrite the cost of developing the next generation of semiconductor technologies—in other words, for replacing the hidden industrial policy of military procurement with a new post-Cold War technology development initiative (NACS 1992).

It is in this context of heightened concern about the competitiveness of the U.S. semiconductor industry that this book is written. My purpose is to reexamine the structure of manufacturing systems and the terms of competition characteristic of semiconductor production within the United States by investigating the basis for the sustained innovative dynamism of the industry as well as the limits and liabilities of emergent manufacturing forms. Much has been written about the early history of the industry, and in particular about the emergence of Silicon Valley during the 1960s and 1970s as the dominant center of semiconductor manufacturing in the United States. Less is known about the more recent development of the industry during the 1980s. Discussion of semiconductors and other high-technology industries is now dominated by the rise to market leadership of Japan. The focus on Japan, however, has tended to overshadow important changes that are now occurring in the organization and geography of the U.S. semiconductor industry. Drawing on the results of new case-study research on the U.S. semiconductor industry, this book provides empirical and conceptual analysis of the changing structure of semiconductor manufacturing in the United States. The analysis is based on detailed information obtained from U.S. firms through a series of interviews and questionnaire surveys conducted over the period 1989–91.

In the mid-1980s semiconductor manufacturing in the

United States was an industry with both strengths and weaknesses. The basic infrastructure of research laboratories and universities remained unmatched throughout the world, generating a host of technological breakthroughs and a large supply of highly trained engineers and scientists. The innovative dynamism of Silicon Valley start-up firms continued unabated, unleashing a stream of new products and market applications. At the same time, however, U.S. semiconductor firms were plagued by persistent problems of low yields in production, poor manufacturing quality, and fluctuating capacity utilization. These problems were experienced by most U.S. firms and reflected fundamental weaknesses in semiconductor manufacturing practices in the United States. The root of the production difficulties was a narrow conception of technological change: the latter was interpreted almost exclusively as an issue of research and product development rather than as a dynamic influencing all aspects of the manufacturing process. Production problems among U.S. firms provided the crucial point of entry for Japanese competitors, allowing the latter to break into foreign markets and capture substantial dynamic learning economies in advanced integrated circuit production.

An analysis written in the late 1980s would likely have ended here, echoing the pessimistic evaluations of other industry observers. However, it is now clear that the U.S. semiconductor industry is currently undergoing a new round of restructuring that is as remarkable as anything experienced earlier in the history of this sector of production. The most visible aspect of change has been the proliferation of partnership agreements among semiconductor firms; the semiconductor industry worldwide is rapidly becoming dominated by formalized global and local networks of firms linked together through technology development, production, and cooperative research agreements. The traditional Schumpeterian dualism of the entrepreneur and the large firm is rapidly being replaced by new organizational forms centered on networks of small and large firms. Of equal importance have been changes in the internal manufacturing operations of many U.S. semiconductor firms, from the restructuring of basic research activities to changes in relations with equipment manufacturers, customers, and suppliers. Processes of industrial restructuring have substantially enhanced the manufacturing performance of U.S. firms, improving product quality, production yields, and time-to-market for new technologies. These changes constitute nothing less than a remaking of the U.S. semiconductor industry.

To some degree the current round of restructuring is driven by processes specific to the semiconductor industry. With the widespread transition of semiconductor manufacturing to ever greater levels of miniaturization and circuit integration (and in particular to submicron production), the costs of design and fabrication have increased dramatically. High-volume fabrication facilities for submicron devices now cost in excess of $300 million to construct and equip. Development costs for the next generation of Dynamic Random Access Memory (DRAM) integrated circuits are expected to exceed $1 billion. In the face of escalating R&D and capital equipment costs during the 1980s, semiconductor firms have sought ways of sharing the expense and risks of developing new technology, including the establishment of various cooperative research and production agreements. New design technologies (such as advanced compilers and board simulators) and new methods for manufacturing semiconductors (such as application-specific technologies) have emerged that substantially alter the structure of economies of scale and scope within the industry.

The current reorganization of the semiconductor industry, however, also reflects a more general series of developments in the structure of interfirm competition and the character of manufacturing systems within advanced industrial economies. In the context of intensified international competition, firms and industries are seeking new sources of profit and durable competitive advantage. In semiconductors, and apparently in many other sectors of production, manufacturing systems are increasingly being recentered on a dynamic of *continuous innovation* in which competitive advantage is based on the ability to develop and deploy new technologies and attendant work practices ahead of competitors. In an era of intensified global competition, it is the ability to anticipate and create new market opportunities, to develop new products ahead of competitors, and to reconfigure manufacturing processes rapidly in response to changing production requirements that offers the best prospect for long-term profitability of firms and industries. Once viewed as merely one aspect of the manufacturing process, the capacity to sustain innovation in technology, work practices, and product markets is now the central regulatory problem for semiconductor firms, and a primary determinant of the organizational and geographical structure of manufacturing in the semiconductor industry.

The ongoing restructuring of the U.S. semiconductor industry for continuous innovation has already had a substantial impact on the competitiveness of U.S. producers in global markets, and more generally on the pattern of competition and cooperation among U.S., Japanese, and European semiconductor firms. The dire predictions of the mid-1980s that anticipated an accelerated decline of U.S. firms to the point where Japan would dominate in most leading-edge product markets have not come to pass. Indeed, preliminary data suggest that in 1992 the United States surpassed Japan in semiconductor shipments, thereby reassuming (at least temporarily) the position of largest producer of semiconductors in the world. Learning from their Japanese competitors, U.S. firms have instituted sweeping changes in manufacturing practice that have dramatically narrowed the gap between the two countries in production quality, yields, and output cost. This "Japanization" of U.S. manufacturing practice, involving, for example, much closer ties between semiconductor firms, equipment suppliers, and subcontractors, has slowed the loss of existing markets to foreign competitors. At the same time, an accelerated rate of product and process-technology development has allowed U.S. firms to sustain a leadership position in many highly profitable new product lines, such as advanced microprocessors, flash memories, and high-density field programmable gate arrays.

Much of the recent debate concerning the competitive prospects of the U.S. semiconductor industry has turned on the relative merits of large and small firms. It is important to note in this regard that it is large and medium-size semiconductor firms—most notably IBM, Intel, Motorola, and Texas Instruments—that have been the leading agents of change in

manufacturing practice within the U.S. semiconductor industry. To a significant degree, it is the ability of these large
producers to improve yields and accelerate the pace of product
development that has allowed the United States to increase its
share of high-value product markets. This is not to suggest that
the entrepreneurial patterns of industrialization observed in
Silicon Valley have become incidental to the innovative dynamism of the U.S. semiconductor industry. Small start-up firms
continue to play a crucial role in rapidly exploiting new technologies and identifying new market opportunities. However
few small firms stand alone; the majority are now bound into a
complex array of cooperative alliances with large established
producers. While the final configuration of these cooperative
linkages is far from clear, the Schumpeterian dualism of entrepreneur and large firm appears to be giving way to a
new organizational model in which large firms serve as an-
chors for a shifting network of alliances and manufacturing
agreements.

The most likely scenario for the semiconductor industry
over the next decade is a stabilization of U.S. and Japanese
global market share at or close to current levels. Only the most
optimistic analysts would have made such a prediction five
years ago, when U.S. market share was in free fall and Japanese
competitors seemed poised to expand into new high-value markets. Improvements in U.S. manufacturing performance, and
the limited success of Japanese firms at diversifying into new
design-intensive product markets, are the central economic
processes underlying the stabilization of market share. At the
same time, an emergent politics of balanced trade relations
between the United States and Japan will likely provide additional support to U.S. firms by enhancing access to Japanese
markets. Stabilization of U.S. market share is dependent,
however, on ongoing improvement in manufacturing yields,
product quality, and turnaround time for new technologies.
The trajectory of industrial restructuring initiated during
the late 1980s must be continued through the 1990s and beyond.

Even as stabilization of the economic fortunes of the U.S.
semiconductor industry has occurred, it has become clear that

emergent manufacturing forms are characterized by a profoundly different mix of global competition and cooperation than that which characterized semiconductor production through the mid-1980s. The new institutional structure of innovation and technology development in semiconductors involves a complex array of international cooperative alliances and research agreements among U.S., Japanese, and European firms. To a significant degree, the primary axis of competition in the 1990s will no longer be between Japan and the United States, but between competing global networks of producers, such as that of IBM, Siemens, and Toshiba, or the alliance for long-term technology development between AT&T and NEC. This globalization of semiconductor manufacturing has profound implications for national technology initiatives, such as that maintained by MITI in Japan, or that of Sematech in the United States. It also raises important questions concerning processes of regional development. As I will attempt to show, the current proliferation of global technology alliances notwithstanding, there remain important territorial dimensions to processes of innovation and technology development in semiconductors that are likely to ensure the continued concentration of technology development in a limited number of specialized agglomerations around the globe.

RESTRUCTURING FOR INNOVATION

All organizations face the dilemma of balancing their relative orientation to efficiency and to innovation. For much of the twentieth century, there has been a tendency to give efficiency a priority over innovation, but this tendency began to alter in the 1970s. Today innovation is surpassing efficiency as the primary principle for deciding the most appropriate form of organization. (Clark and Staunton 1989, p. 3)

It is now widely acknowledged that the past thirty years have been a period of profound change in the structure of manufacturing systems within advanced capitalist economies. Economic change has involved the development of new products and production processes, as well as new ways of organizing work and new patterns of employment and labor relations. In the face of declining profits and intensified international competition, firms and industries are now attempting to secure new sources of durable competitive advantage. The hegemony of established manufacturing forms, such as that associated with the mass production of automobiles and other consumer durables during the midpart of the twentieth century, is increasingly being undermined by a variety of new and previously marginalized production systems.

For a growing number of authors, these processes of industrial change are best understood in terms of a search for greater flexibility in the manufacturing system (Gertler 1988, 1992; Piore and Sabel 1984; Sabel 1989; Schoenberger 1989; Scott 1988a). As discussions of flexibility have proliferated within the literature, however, the concept has tended to lose clear conceptual and empirical definition; used to describe multiple dimensions of different manufacturing systems, the concept retains little clear meaning. The term flexibility has been variously used to describe specific automated manufacturing technologies, labor relations (Pollert 1988), vertically disintegrated organizational forms (flexible specialization), institutions of economic regulation (flexible accumulation), as well as a postmodern and antiessentialist orientation to political economic theory (Hirst and Zeitlin 1991).[1]

Much of the initial case-study work on flexible production systems centered on a hypothesized collapse of mass markets into multiple niche and segmented markets, and an attendant shift in manufacturing systems away from the dedicated machinery typical of routinized mass production lines (Scott 1988b; Storper and Christopherson 1987). By this account, the

---

[1]The absence of conceptual clarity has generated more heated debate than systematic empirical analysis (Amin and Robins 1990; Lovering 1991). Measurement of the extent to which a transition to flexibility is taking place is confounded by multiple definitions of what constitutes flexibility in the production system. Most of the celebrated case study examples of flexible specialization (such as the Third Italy) involve production systems centered on localized networks of small, vertically disintegrated firms. Proponents of the flexibility thesis suggest, however, that flexible specialization is only one of a variety of potential organizational and institutional forms. By this account, the tendency toward flexibility is defined less in terms of a specific organizational and territorial structure than in terms of the ability of firms and industries to reconfigure production resources rapidly and at low cost in response to changing market demand.

key feature of emerging production systems has been the enhanced capability of firms to change production volumes and to make rapid alterations in product/process configurations in response to changing consumer demands. Such flexibility is achieved in part through the use of automated programmable production and assembly equipment. Often it also involves an extended use of external subcontractors and suppliers as a buffer against changing production volume and product requirements.

While such production flexibility is to be observed in the semiconductor industry and in other high-technology sectors of production, it is appropriately seen as only one expression of a more general process of continuous innovation.[2] The flexibility being sought by manufacturing firms now increasingly extends beyond the ability to vary the volume and configuration of existing production lines to an enhanced capacity to identify and pursue new product markets, to develop new product technologies (rather than simply variations on existing product lines), and to compete over the long term by anticipating and exploiting new economic opportunities ahead of competitors. These dimensions of innovation have, of course, always been one element of interfirm competition within advanced industrial economies. What distinguishes emerging manufacturing systems is that the search for innovative capability is now a primary determinant of the organizational and geographical structure of the production system. While in the past innovation had been treated as a discrete activity, typically confined "offline" and introduced to manufacturing activities only occasionally as part of a major retooling of production lines, it is now becoming central to all aspects of the organization and structure of production systems. The manufacturing system as a whole, from product design through final assembly and test, is optimized for innovation.

---

[2]As Piore (1992) has recently noted, the adoption of programmable production equipment, while reducing the costs of changing product configurations on the production line, does not necessitate the abandonment of mass production. Programmable equipment has been successfully installed within existing high-volume production systems, creating a hybrid manufacturing form that nevertheless retains the basic characteristics of mass production (i.e., a commitment to economies of scale, detailed division of labor, and a separation of conception and execution in production). Piore labels this manufacturing form "flexible mass production."

Notions of accelerated innovation—variously referred to as perpetual innovation, concurrent engineering, time-based competition, and so forth (Drucker 1990; Gomory 1989; Gupta and Wileman 1990)—have been present in the business management literature for some years. As used here, the concept of continuous innovation refers to manufacturing systems that establish advantage on an ability to develop new products, production processes, and markets ahead of competing firms. The emphasis placed on innovation does not imply the disappearance of other dimensions of interfirm competition, such as price and product reliability. Indeed, it is precisely because of the intensity of competition in the manufacture of existing products, and the attendant low profits in mature product markets, that firms are seeking to enhance their ability to develop new products and production processes whose profit margins are typically much larger. The increasing attention paid to time-to-market for new products, and shortened life cycles for new technologies, is a consequence of the low profit margins achieved by all but the very lowest-cost producers in mature product markets. By being the first to recognize new market opportunities, the first to market new products, and the first to achieve high-yield volume production with new devices, firms are able to secure much higher rates of return on investment, a prerequisite of long-term survival in competitive global markets.

The reorientation of manufacturing systems around a dynamic of continuous innovation is a key element of the contemporary restructuring process in advanced industrial economies. This is not to suggest, however, that other manufacturing strategies have been totally marginalized within the economy. Clearly, alternative strategies abound, including attempting to enhance profitability through the routinization of production processes and the increased use of low-wage labor. Moreover, in industries whose profit margins remain strong as a result of high barriers-to-entry or other sources of monopolistic advantage, the tendency to restructure is correspondingly muted. Across a wide spectrum of industrial sectors, however, the rapid diffusion of technological knowledge and manufacturing capability has created new competitors and eroded profit margins on existing products and production processes.[3] Under these conditions of intensified competition, continuous innovation offers one of the best prospects for achieving durable competitive advantage.

The concept of continuous innovation does not imply that product development is given priority over high-quality production; rather, continuous innovation is characterized by an ability to sustain high-quality low-cost production under conditions of rapidly changing markets and technology. As Florida and Kenney (1990a) have indicated, much of the loss of market share experienced by U.S. high-technology firms during the 1980s derived not from a shortage of innovative capability, but from notoriously poor production yields and low production quality. These production problems arose in part from a fundamental tension between the drive to reduce costs on existing products, and pressures to introduce new products and production processes. The dominant tendency in existing high-technology manufacturing systems has been toward a linear and fragmented model of manufacturing, in which innovation is treated as a discrete activity, one organizationally and geographically separate from production. Emerging production forms, by contrast, are characterized by a reintegration of innovation and production, and of conception and execution, within the manufacturing system. Thus, much of the attention of semiconductor firms seeking to accelerate the time-to-market for new products is now focused not in the research laboratory but on the factory floor; the ability to stabilize new technologies in production, and then to ramp up rapidly to high-yield production, is central to the process of continuous innovation.

The concept of continuous innovation proposed here involves a significant extension of the notions of flexibility used in much of the widely cited case-study research. In particular, the analysis places increased emphasis on sources of innovation within the manufacturing system, that is, on the development

---

[3]In the case of high-technology industries, this tendency is seen most clearly in terms of the rise of South Korea, Singapore, and Taiwan as major industrial powers. Mechanisms for the rapid international transfer of technological knowledge include the location of research facilities in foreign countries; strategic alliances among firms; investment in, and purchase of, leading-edge high-technology firms; and the large enrollment of foreign students in American universities.

of new technologies, work practices, and product ideas. To date, the majority of case studies of flexible production systems have focused on the ability of firms to manufacture different products, to change production volumes, and to reconfigure manufacturing resources in response to new market demands. The processes whereby these new products, production technologies, and market ideas are developed have only rarely been addressed. Indeed, in some formulations of flexibility and post-Fordism, enhanced innovative capability is specifically excluded from analysis (Sayer 1989).

Despite a large and growing literature on innovation (see, for example, the recent work by Dosi [1988, 1990] and Rosenberg [1982]), issues of innovation and technology development remain marginal in current debates concerning the durability of flexible manufacturing forms. The major exception is the growing interest in the role of production networks in innovation (Aydalot and Keeble 1988; Camagni 1991; Freeman 1992; Storper 1992). It is now widely recognized that the highly centralized, vertically integrated organizational forms characteristic of mass production during the middle part of the twentieth century are poorly suited to the emerging competitive conditions of continuous innovation, frequent market shifts, and rapid technological change.[4] Such established manufacturers as G.E., Hewlett Packard, and IBM are moving rapidly to restructure their manufacturing operations, whether for computers or semiconductors. Much of the restructuring involves changes within the firm, such as decentralization of decision making and increased dependence on multidimensional product teams as the primary agents of innovation and new technology development. In many cases, however, restructuring also involves significant externalization of manufacturing activities as well as increased dependence on external sources of technological knowledge and production capability. Typically, such externalization involves the establish-

---

[4]The downsizing and decentralization of large corporations should not be interpreted as the triumph of the small firm. Rather, large firms are transforming their organizational structure in ways that allow them to retain market power under conditions of intensified competition, rapid technological change, and uncertain and fluctuating demand.

ment of network relations among firms, whether in the form of strategic alliances and partnership agreements or in the form of informal cooperation and mutual dependence.

Innovation and flexibility are now closely intertwined on the factory floor; hence, there is an important need to bring these two themes together in the analysis of contemporary manufacturing systems and industrial change. This requires an examination of both formalized R&D activities and informal processes of learning and information exchange within and among firms. A key element of contemporary restructuring and continuous innovation is the attempt to reduce the cost of learning and accelerate the pace at which information flows within the manufacturing system. This attempt involves changes in organizational form and a fundamental restructuring of the labor process and attendant employment relations. It is also likely to involve important changes in the geography of manufacturing systems. Of particular interest here is the possibility that the drive to accelerate information flows will contribute to an intensified regionalization of production systems within a series of specialized industrial agglomerations or industrial districts. As Dosi (1988) and others have indicated, "many of the opportunities for technological development and the capacity to pursue them are distinctly local and regional in character." Much technological knowledge is of a tacit kind, embedded in the skills and experiences of workers, institutions, and communities, and not easily transferable across national and regional boundaries.

The analysis presented here suggests the need for a broader investigation of market demand as an internal element of the manufacturing system, an element created and structured as one part of the process of innovation. As a number of observers have suggested (see, for example, Haslam 1987), much of the initial case study research on flexible production systems has tended to treat the changing structure of markets (the segmentation of mass markets and the proliferation of low-volume and specialized market niches) as an external phenomenon, a dynamic that firms have responded to rather than created. This book shows that the creation and management of market demand is a central internal moment within the dynamic of continuous innovation: the ability of firms to continually develop and deploy new technologies is dependent on a parallel capability to create and sustain uses for these technologies (i.e., through the codevelopment of new software and new electronics systems, and the establishment of industry standards for emerging technologies). Continuous innovation requires the simultaneous and coordinated generation of new technologies and new markets, and the ability to manufacture profitably under these conditions of rapid technological and market change.

These ideas echo themes from the work of several commentators on high-technology industrialization in the United States. Johnson, Tyson, and Zysman (1989) draw attention to an orientation toward "Schumpeterian efficiency" among Japanese semiconductor firms; the organizational and investment decisions of many of these firms are apparently based on a desire to enhance the technology development process rather than simply the cost efficiency of existing products and production processes. Similarly, Florida and Kenney (1992) argue persuasively for the need to bridge the gap between innovation and production (conception and execution) within high-technology manufacturing systems. None of these authors, however, have anticipated the range and the character of response to international competition implemented by U.S. semiconductor firms during the 1980s. Even quite recent evaluations of the industry (Henderson 1989), the majority of which continue to counterpose start-up semiconductor firms in the United States to large, vertically integrated electronics firms in Japan, fail to recognize the extent and significance of recent changes in the organizational and geographical structure of the U.S. semiconductor industry.

The Case of Semiconductors

In the semiconductor industry the dynamic of continuous innovation focuses above all on the development and deployment of new technologies. Much of the current restructuring of the U.S. semiconductor industry may be understood in terms of efforts to reduce the cost and accelerate the speed at which new semiconductor technologies are developed, deployed, and adopted in the marketplace. The dynamic of innovation, however, is not simply a matter of technology development. In addition to new product and process technologies, innovation involves the simultaneous development of new work practices, new markets, and new uses for these technologies.

In many respects, of course, innovation and technology development have been central to competitive success in the semiconductor industry from the very beginning. Since the foundation of the industry in the 1950s, the ability to develop new product and process technologies, to recognize new applications for semiconductors, and to create product technologies that meet these needs have been essential to the profitability of U.S. semiconductor firms. In meeting the goal of product innovation, U.S. semiconductor firms were supremely successful: they developed a wide variety of breakthrough innovations, from memory circuits to the microprocessor. By one account (Morris 1990), during the formative period of the industry U.S. firms were responsible for approximately 85% of all major technological breakthroughs in semiconductor manufacturing. As late as 1980, the United States still had an approximately 60% share (measured by value) of the worldwide market for semiconductor devices.

There is much to be learnt from existing manufacturing systems about organizational and territorial conditions conducive to the development of new technologies. Indeed, it is this aspect of U.S. high-technology industrialization that has garnered the most interest among researchers and policymakers alike. Researchers have identified a series of characteristics of the U.S. economy conducive to high-technology production, including an extensive infrastructure of basic research institutions, strong support from military research and procurement programs, and a large supply of highly skilled engineers and scientists. There is now a large body of research investigating the foundation for the innovative dynamism of Silicon Valley and other specialized high-technology districts (Angel 1989, 1990; Glasmeier 1985; Malecki 1983, 1991; Oakey 1981; Saxenian 1990, 1991), and more generally, the forms of regional and national policy intervention likely to attract and support semiconductor firms (Asher and Strom 1977; Borrus 1988a, 1988b; Borrus, Millstein, and Zysman 1982; Braun and Mac-Donald 1982; Ernst 1983; Ernst and O'Connor 1992; Harrington 1985; Levin 1982; Malerba 1985; Okimoto, Sugano, and Weinstein 1984; Rogers and Larsen 1984; Tilton 1971; United Nations Center on Transnational Corporations [UNCTC] 1986; U.S. Department of Commerce 1979).

To a significant degree, however, the capability for innovation of U.S. semiconductor firms obscured a series of fundamental regulatory and managerial problems in existing manufacturing systems. While U.S. firms excelled in R&D and the development of new products, the actual production and assembly of semiconductor devices was plagued by persistent problems of low yields, poor quality, and fluctuating production capacity utilization. Failure rates of more than 70% were not uncommon on many advanced product lines. Many industry observers initially suggested that these production difficulties were the inevitable result of a complex, multistep, manufacturing process, high levels of miniaturization, and the rapid changes in technology associated with an emerging industry. During the 1980s, however, it became increasingly clear that poor production performance derived in large part from the structure of manufacturing systems in the U.S. semiconductor industry. Throughout the 1960s and 1970s, U.S. semiconductor firms maintained a kind of bifurcated manufacturing system: one segment was oriented toward technology development and problems of innovation, whereas the other segment was focused on production and problems of production cost.

At the root of the problem lay a narrow conception of technological change. Among U.S. semiconductor firms, technological change was interpreted primarily as a matter of innovation and product development, rather than as a dynamic influencing all aspects of the manufacturing process. While manufacturers sought organizational structures and locations that facilitated the development of new products, the actual production of semiconductor devices was organized with little regard to the pattern of rapid technological change that characterized the industry. Production and assembly functions were optimized for the low-cost manufacture of existing products rather than for manufacturing under conditions of rapid technological change. In general, the search for low production cost involved the adoption of manufacturing strategies commonly used by other industries, such as automobiles and consumer electronics, including the construction of dedicated mass-production lines and the extended use of low-cost labor. It also involved a marked spatial division of labor, in which technology development and production activities were geographically separated one from another. While R&D and innovation remained clustered in core locations, production and assembly tasks were shifted to dispersed low-cost locations in the United States and offshore.

Under conditions of rapid technological change, the organizational and geographical separation of production and innovation generated serious and time-consuming difficulties in transferring new technologies from the laboratory to the factory floor. In addition, in the face of rapidly changing product and process technologies, the use of dedicated production lines created tremendous problems for investment and for capacity utilization. Shortages of production capacity for new products were accompanied by excess capacity for older technologies.

As long as U.S. firms maintained a technological advantage over their international rivals, these production difficulties primarily affected profit margins rather than market share. From the mid-1970s onward, however, Japanese firms, under the coordination of the Ministry of International Trade and Industry (MITI), initiated a broadly based effort to reach parity with U.S. firms in semiconductor technology (Johnson 1985). The challenge was initially aimed at the weakest link in the U.S. semiconductor industry, namely, production. Using industry-standard product design and process technology licensed from U.S. firms, Japanese producers achieved substantially higher production yields and improved production quality, and captured a large share of the market for DRAM integrated circuits. Subsequently, Japanese firms established a leadership position in the development of process technology and in key high-volume product markets (above all, in the production of DRAM integrated circuits).

Figure 1.1 shows the shares of semiconductor markets held

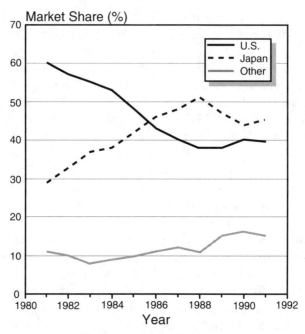

FIGURE 1.1. Estimated shares of worldwide semiconductor markets, 1981–91. (Adapted from Semiconductor Industry Association data.)

by Japanese and U.S. firms during the period 1981–91. By 1986 Japan had surpassed the United States as the largest producer of semiconductors in the world. In 1988 Japanese firms captured more than 50% of the total world market for semiconductors. Japan's rapid penetration of advanced integrated-circuit product markets was the result of a complex of factors, including low capital costs, a protected domestic market, and a willingness at times to sell below production cost in order to capture market share. Underlying much of the success of Japanese firms, however, was a close integration of technology development and production activities, involving frequent rotation of workers from R&D into production, a commitment to solve problems of product qualify on the production line (as opposed to eliminating defective devices during the final test), and a general orientation toward the development of "manufacturable" products (e.g., by designing products that required fewer production steps).

In response to competition from Japan, from the mid-1980s onward the majority of U.S. semiconductor firms initiated a major restructuring of their manufacturing operations in an effort to increase yields and improve production quality. Learning from their Japanese competitors, U.S. firms have focused on establishing closer ties between research, product development, and production. At the same time, this restructuring has involved building closer and more collaborative relations between semiconductor firms and their customers, subcontractors, and equipment suppliers (see Stowsky 1989 for a critique of the relations between U.S. semiconductor firms and their equipment manufacturers). These actions have substantially improved manufacturing performance. While the yields of Japanese semiconductor firms remain somewhat higher than those of their U.S. competitors (a result, in part, of the much greater automation of production in Japanese fabrication facilities), the gap has substantially narrowed. The ability of U.S. firms to improve yields and production quality has served to dispel much of the aura of mystique surrounding Japan's performance in high-technology industries. That it took a major crisis of profitability to bring forth these changes is indicative of the deep entrenchment of existing manufacturing practice within U.S. semiconductor firms.

Information on manufacturing yields and product quality is closely guarded by semiconductor firms. Two sets of data provide evidence, however, of the substantial improvements in manufacturing performance achieved by U.S. firms during the second half of the 1980s. The first set of data is the information collected by the Semiconductor Industry Association on the frequency of defects in integrated circuits manufactured for military applications. Military users require stringent quality testing of semiconductor devices; the results of these tests provide considerable insight into changes in the manufacturing capability of U.S. semiconductor firms. Product defects declined from an average of 170–190 parts-per-million in 1986, to an average of 50–60 parts-per-million in 1990 (Kendrick 1992).

The second set of data is contained in a recent report of the U.S. General Accounting Office assessing the impact of

Sematech on the U.S. semiconductor industry (U.S. GAO 1992). These data compare the wafer probe yields achieved by U.S. and Japanese firms, based on information provided by the consulting firm VLSI Research.[5] Probe yields of U.S. firms increased from 60% in 1986, to 84% in 1991. During the same period, yields achieved by Japanese firms increased from 75% to 93%. Thus, while Japanese firms continue to maintain higher manufacturing performance than that of U.S. producers, the difference in yields between the two groups of firms has narrowed from 15% in 1986, to 9% in 1991. This reduction in the yield differential substantially enhanced the ability of U.S. firms to compete with Japanese producers during the late 1980s.

Improvements in the quality of manufacturing are only one aspect of the contemporary restructuring process in the global semiconductor industry. Even with improved yields, profits on most mature product lines have remained relatively thin for all semiconductor firms. Moreover, from the late 1980s onward, profit margins for DRAMs and other high-volume products have narrowed further with the entry of South Korea as an additional competitor. Following the example of Japanese firms in the early 1980s, Korean producers have focused on capturing market share, thereby placing intense downward pressure on prices for DRAM devices. Since initiating DRAM production in the late 1980s, using technology licensed from Japan, South Korean firms have gone on to capture approximately 20% of the worldwide market for DRAM devices. Under these conditions of intensified international competition, both Japanese *and* U.S. semiconductor firms are placing increased emphasis on new products and production processes, seeking ways to shorten the time-to-market for new technologies whose the return on investment is greater. It is this competitive dynamic that underlies the reorientation to continuous innovation. In a drive to accelerate technology development, semiconductor firms are now attempting to reintegrate and recentralize manufacturing systems around a core of ongoing innovation. This is a process that is influencing all aspects of the semiconductor industry, from the internal organization of

[5]Wafer probe is an electrical test performed on semiconductors prior to final assembly.

semiconductor firms, to relations with customers, sub-contractors, and suppliers. It is also a process that is having important implications for the geography of production: to a significant degree, locational decisions are now driven not by factor input costs but by issues of communication and learning that are central to the emerging dynamic of innovation. Attempts to enhance the development and deployment of new technologies, and to create new markets, are supporting both locational reconcentration (e.g., the co-location of technology development and production activities within the same facilities) and increasing globalization of manufacturing activities (as firms seek to enhance their capability to meet the needs of different national markets).

The declining fortune of the United States in many high-technology industries has stimulated widespread debate among academics and policymakers about political, organizational, and territorial forms most conducive to the rapid development and deployment of new technologies. At the center of the policy debate is the structure of the U.S. semiconductor industry. The research reported here suggests that the long-standing targets of debate, from the underfunded start-up firm to the slow-moving bureaucratized corporate giant, are rapidly being replaced by new organizational and geographical forms, and by manufacturing systems centered on a competitive dynamic of continuous innovation. To a significant degree, the durability of emerging manufacturing forms will depend on the ability of firms to resolve the diversity of regulatory problems associated with production under conditions of rapid change in markets and technology. The remainder of the book is devoted to a detailed case study analysis of the strategies used by U.S. firms to meet these challenges, and of the implications of the restructuring process for the location of semiconductor manufacturing through the 1990s and beyond.

ORGANIZATION OF THE BOOK

Chapter 2 presents a historical overview of the development of manufacturing systems in the U.S. semiconductor industry,

and of the organizational and geographical structure of semiconductor production in the United States. Much has been
written about the early history of the industry, the period from
the late 1940s through the 1960s. Accordingly, the focus here is
on the most recent period of rapid growth and intensified
global competition, from the early 1970s onwards. The objective is to identify the basis for the rapid rise to dominance of the
United States in semiconductors, and to identify sources of
structural weakness in the manufacturing forms that emerged
in the U.S. semiconductor industry. Of particular interest is the
contribution of Silicon Valley to the competitive success of the
United States in semiconductors. Silicon Valley start-up firms
have played a key role in identifying and exploiting new technological and market opportunities. The entrepreneurial activity of start-up firms has always depended, however, on a broader technology-development infrastructure, including the R&D
activities of large, established firms.

Chapter 3 examines the changing fortunes of the U.S.
semiconductor industry under conditions of intensified global
competition from the late 1970s onward. The Japanese challenge to U.S. market dominance is examined in detail, including both the role of MITI and the subsequent sources of competitive advantage established by Japanese firms. In addition, I
examine the initial response of U.S. firms to the Japanese
challenge during the early 1980s. In the face of intensified
international competition, weaknesses in existing manufacturing practice were rapidly exposed. Aspects of existing technology-development practice that were previously a source of
competitive advantage (such as the tendency toward an "open"
technology environment) now emerged as a source of competitive weakness.

Chapters 4 and 5 provide detailed empirical analysis of the
restructuring of manufacturing systems in the U.S. semiconductor industry from the mid-1980s onward. The analysis is
based on new original data collected by questionnaire survey
and in-depth interviews with engineers and senior managerial
staff of U.S. semiconductor firms. A series of surveys and
interviews was conducted during the period 1989–91. Chapter
4 focuses on the pattern of response to global competition

instituted by U.S. semiconductor firms. Two themes emerge. The first is the increasing "Japanization" of semiconductor manufacturing practice in the United States, as revealed, for example, in closer ties between semiconductor producers and equipment suppliers. The second theme is the integration of innovation and production within U.S. semiconductor firms; this integration replaces a previously fragmented manufacturing form and allows for improved manufacturing performance and a more rapid deployment of new technologies. A series of different manufacturing strategies are also described, ranging from an emphasis on so-called value-added manufacturing, in which competitive advantage is rooted in the quality of the circuit design, to an emphasis on leading-edge process technology. In addition, I examine the specific strategies used by U.S. semiconductor firms to accelerate the development of new technology, focusing on the case of leading-edge submicron process technology.

Chapter 5 investigates a second dimension of industrial restructuring, namely, the proliferation of strategic alliances and partnership agreements between semiconductor firms. Few semiconductor firms now stand alone; most are enmeshed in a complex array of technology development, production, and marketing agreements. Underlying these organizational changes is a series of developments in markets and in production technology that has profoundly changed the preexisting structure of economies of scale and scope in the semiconductor industry. Of particular significance have been the rising cost of technology development, and the tendency toward market and technology specialization on the part of many semiconductor firms. In practice, many of the alliances formed in the semiconductor industry are international in scope, raising fears of an accelerated diffusion of advanced technology to foreign competitors and of job loss in the U.S. semiconductor industry. Many of the initial alliances between U.S. and foreign firms were poorly structured, marked by a largely one-way flow of technology and information, and by a tendency for collaborative relations to collapse into competition. To a significant degree, however, U.S. firms have learnt from this experience, and recent technology partnerships, such as that between IBM, Siemens, and Toshiba, are likely to enhance rather than undermine the competitiveness of U.S. semiconductor firms.

Chapter 6 is devoted to an examination of the role of government institutions in supporting the U.S. semiconductor industry, including an assessment of the contribution of Sematech and the 1986 U.S.–Japan Trade Agreement to the stabilization of U.S. market share during the late 1980s. For much of the 1980s the semiconductor industry was at the center of a wide ranging policy debate on the desirability of targeted government support for industries experiencing competitive difficulties. My analysis suggests that while Sematech and the market access provisions of the Trade Agreement have helped to increase the competitiveness of the U.S. semiconductor industry, their contribution in this regard has been largely secondary to the efforts made by semiconductor firms themselves to improve manufacturing performance and enhance technology-development capability.

The book concludes with an assessment of the likely implications of contemporary processes of restructuring for the location of U.S semiconductor firms, and, more generally, for high-technology industrialization in the United States.

REPRISE

For more than three decades the semiconductor industry has fascinated economic analysts. Of all the new industries—from artificial intelligence to biotechnology—none has matched the ability of the semiconductor industry to capture the interest and imagination of academics, planners, and policymakers alike. To a significant degree, this attention reflects the status of semiconductors as an emergent foundational technology for industrial systems: semiconductors are akin to steam power and the internal combustion engine in supporting a new trajectory of industrial development and in offering the possibility of renewed growth, improvements in productivity, and qualitatively different ways of addressing the enduring material needs of societies.

The widespread diffusion of semiconductor technology has already had a profound effect on many aspects of life, from health care to warfare. Several authors have suggested that semiconductors provide the foundation for a new techno-economic paradigm that will redefine the path of global economic change and development (Dosi 1982; Freeman 1987; Perez 1985). Attempts to grasp the character of this age of solid-state electronics and its significance for such diverse concerns as the environment, privacy, and security, are still in their infancy.

The foundational status of semiconductors is not the only reason for interest in this industry however. Attention also derives from a belief that in several important respects the manufacture of semiconductors represents a break with previously dominant patterns of industrialization in advanced economies, drawing on new types of knowledge and labor skills, and potentially providing a new basis for durable regional economic growth and development. Semiconductors are representative of an emergent ensemble of science-intensive and technology-intensive industries; competitive advantage in these industries is increasingly determined not by wages or other factor-input costs, but by the quality of scientific and engineering resources, and by the ability of firms, regions, and nations to deploy these resources effectively in the development of new products and production processes. By the same token, the foundations of national and regional competitive advantage in technology-intensive industries are not pregiven, as is the case with natural resource endowments, but actively constructed as part of the process of industrial and social development (Krugman 1991). The search for organizational and territorial forms that facilitate technological development and science-based innovation has involved a rejection of many of the hitherto-accepted industrial practices as well as many previously hegemonic manufacturing forms.

Nowhere has there been greater interest in the industry than in the United States, where the development of semiconductor manufacturing has coincided with a period of profound instability and job loss in many older industries, such as textiles and steel. Figure 1.2 shows graphically the changes in employment in the semiconductor and other selected industries during the period 1966–89. These data indicate that after especially rapid growth in the late 1970s, U.S. employment in the semiconductor industry totaled 158,104 in 1980, and 188,809 in 1989. Glasmeier (1991) reports that during the period 1972–82 total U.S. employment in high-technology industries increased by 1,221,726. This rapid expansion in high-technology employment stands in marked contrast to the loss of manufacturing jobs in such mature industries as woven textiles, shipbuilding, and steel. In the latter three industries, the United States experienced a net loss of more than 540,000 jobs during the period 1966–89 (see Figure 1.2).

The growth of the semiconductor industry led many analysts in the 1970s to interpret industrial change as a process of

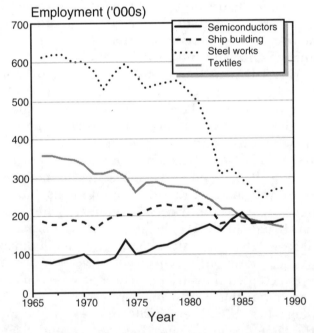

FIGURE 1.2. U.S. employment in semiconductor and selected industries, 1966–89 (Adapted from U.S. Department of Commerce, Bureau of the Census. 1966–89. *Census of Manufactures.* Washington, DC: U.S. Government Printing Office.)

sectoral restructuring; even as production of "low" technology goods shifted to low-wage locations elsewhere in the global economy, new jobs were being created in burgeoning high-technology sectors of production. The success of Silicon Valley start-up firms, many of which were led by young engineers and scientists, served to underscore the impression that the semiconductor industry offered a new and qualitatively different model for industrial and regional development. In the face of economic decline and the loss of manufacturing jobs in older industrial regions, Silicon Valley was widely viewed as a blueprint for new economic growth, a model of entrepreneurial industrialization fueled by venture capital and centered on networks of start-up firms, to be "cloned" elsewhere in the United States and in other advanced industrial economies. Geographically distant from the older industrial centers of the U.S. Manufacturing Belt, Silicon Valley has been emblematic of new possibilities for employment growth and regional development in the United States (Scott and Angel 1987, 1988).

It might be argued that the centrality of innovation in the semiconductor industry is simply a reflection of the youth of the industry, or an expression of the opportunities for innovation inherent in the basic technology. My analysis rejects such technologically deterministic accounts of industrial growth and change (see also Storper and Walker 1989). The semiconductor industry and other high-technology sectors of production are distinguished from older industries by the types of knowledge, labor skills, and material inputs involved in the labor process; all of these industrial sectors operate under the common constraints and contradictions of capitalist accumulation. The current tendency toward accelerated innovation arises out of a profound and widely experienced crisis of profitability in manufacturing systems in advanced industrial economies. At the root of the crisis is an extension of advanced technology and manufacturing capability to an ever larger number of firms, regions, and national economies, and an attendant attenuation of profit margins on existing product technologies (Reich 1991).

The pattern of rapid technological change in the semiconductor industry is the product of complex social, economic, and political conditions. Above all else, it arises out of the phenomenal economic incentives associated with the development of new technology, and the superprofits available to successful firms. Throughout the 1960s and 1970s, the semiconductor industry attracted a massive influx of capital investment, scientific and engineering skills, and managerial competence that advanced the technological frontier at a rapid pace. Precisely because of the pattern of innovation and rapid technological change, the semiconductor industry has been something of a laboratory within which to explore manufacturing forms conducive to the accelerated development and deployment of new technologies. The knowledge and experience generated within this sector concerning production under conditions of rapid change in markets and technology is now being absorbed into the manufacturing practice of other industries, such as automobiles and steel. The significance of the present study thus extends beyond the narrow sectoral concerns of the semiconductor industry, and is of general relevance to the analysis of contemporary processes of restructuring in advanced industrial economies.

CHAPTER 2

The U.S. Semiconductor Industry: Growth and Development

T his chapter provides an overview of the growth and development of the U.S. semiconductor industry. Any analysis of the contemporary realignment of the global semiconductor industry must be rooted in an understanding of the competitive success and technological dominance sustained by U.S. firms through the late 1970s. By the same token, historical analysis of this period of rapid growth reveals structural weaknesses in U.S. semiconductor manufacturing that subsequently provided the crucial point-of-entry for Japan and other foreign competitors.

Since its inception in the late 1940s, the U.S. semiconductor industry has been characterized by a remarkable rate of innovation and growth. U.S. semiconductor shipments increased from $1.7 billion in 1971, to more than $22.0 billion in 1989. To a significant degree, the growth of the industry, and the rapid diffusion of semiconductors throughout many segments of the economy, rest on a continuing pattern of innovation in technology and work practices. Technology development has reduced dramatically the cost and performance of electronic systems and created a multitude of new uses and markets for semiconductor technology. Contrary to the expectations of many industry observers who anticipated a slowdown over time in the rate of technological change, the semiconductor industry continues to exhibit a pattern of short

product life cycles, rapid obsolescence of production technologies and manufacturing equipment, and continuous development of new product configurations and market opportunities. Indeed, as profit margins on existing products have
declined, time-to-market for new technologies has emerged as
a key element of interfirm competition, drawing additional
resources to the innovation process within the semiconductor
industry and enhancing the prospects for the development of
new technologies.

While there is much fascination with technology for its own
sake, processes of innovation are of interest here precisely
because they provide an analytical point-of-entry for understanding general patterns of organizational and geographical
restructuring in manufacturing systems. My argument can be
summarized as follows. The changing fortunes of the U.S.
semiconductor industry—both the success of the 1960s and
1970s, and the declining market share of the 1980s—derive in
large part from the ways in which U.S. firms have dealt (or
failed to deal) with regulatory and managerial problems associated with rapid technological change. In general, the manufacturing systems that emerged in the U.S. semiconductor
industry have been extremely successful in developing new
products and production processes and in identifying new uses
for semiconductor technologies. Throughout most of the
1970s, U.S. semiconductor firms sustained a marked technological edge over all international competitors. By the end of
the decade, however, the failure of U.S. semiconductor firms to
address the full implications of rapid technological change for
the manufacturing system as whole became increasingly clear.
The challenge emerged first at the weakest link, namely, production, where the recurrent problems of low yields and
fluctuating capacity-utilization were experienced by U.S. semiconductor firms. More recently, U.S. firms have experienced a
dramatic erosion of their technological advantage in many
product markets.

My examination of these issues begins with an analysis of
the structure of manufacturing systems as they emerged in the
U.S. semiconductor industry during the period of rapid growth
beginning in the late 1960s. The analysis focuses on the major

characteristics of emergent manufacturing systems. Braun and MacDonald (1982) and Tilton (1971), among others, provide a more detailed historiography of the development of different products and production processes in the industry.

TECHNOLOGY AND MARKET LEADERSHIP

Until the late 1970s, U.S. semiconductor firms dominated the global semiconductor industry. U.S. producers in 1980 still held a nearly 60% share of worldwide open market sales of semiconductor devices. How did this commercial and technological dominance come about?

Two general theoretical perspectives can be identified. The first suggests that technological leadership in semiconductors and other high-technology industries is the result of a cumulative growth process initiated by large-scale investments in science and engineering made in the United States during the middle part of the twentieth century. The second perspective, neo-Schumpeterian in orientation, argues that while the scale and timing of investment is of importance, there are substantial organizational and geographical dimensions to the innovation process that underlie much of the success of U.S. semiconductor firms.

Semiconductors and the National Innovation System

Economic and institutional features that lead to differences between nations as well as between firms in technology development remain only poorly understood (Landau and Rosenberg 1986; Mowery and Rosenberg 1989a). In the case of the semiconductor and other high-technology industries, it is clear that the initial rise to dominance of U.S. firms was the product of a huge expansion in science and engineering investments initiated during the Second World War and maintained during the next three decades. Support for the development of new technology took a number of forms, from government sponsorship of basic research, to the training of engineers and scientists and the creation of markets for leading-edge devices. Much of this science and engineering infrastructure was defense-related, the product of the "hidden" industrial policy of military procurement and government-sponsored R&D (Markusen, Hall, Campbell, and Deitrick 1991).

Semiconductors were a key element of this emergent high-technology complex. Detailed historical data on the scale of research, the investments in training, the size of the labor pool, and other aspects of the technology infrastructure are unavailable for the early years of the industry. We do know that R&D expenditures specifically devoted to the development of semiconductor technology were initially quite small. Tilton (1971) reports a total of $70.2 million spent in 1959. Investments in semiconductors increased rapidly from the early 1960s onward. Total R&D on semiconductors performed by U.S. firms, including both government- and private-sponsored research, grew to more than $800 million at the end of the 1970s, and to in excess of $4 billion at the end of the 1980s.

The development of semiconductors was in practice the result not just of targeted R&D, but also of a more general process of investment in science and engineering in the United States. Semiconductor firms benefitted from extensive basic research and training carried out in the fields of physics, materials chemistry, lithography, and electronics. In addition, R&D investments in allied industries, such as radio, radar, and television, created a market-pull effect on the development of new semiconductor technology. Much of the basic research underlying emergent semiconductor technologies was carried out in the research laboratories of U.S. firms.

Figure 2.1 shows total R&D expenditures in the U.S. and other advanced industrial economies during the period 1961–89. These data indicate that R&D investments in the United States far exceeded those in Japan, the former West Germany, and France.[1] Much of this R&D expenditure was made by the electronics and other high-technology industries. During the

[1] I do not intend to imply here that leadership in high-technology industries is simply a function of R&D investments. The rise to dominance of the United States in semiconductors was the result of research investment, the creation of markets, labor supply, and the institutional structure of innovation. R&D expenditures are cited here as a proxy for the emergence of this totality of science- and technology-based activity.

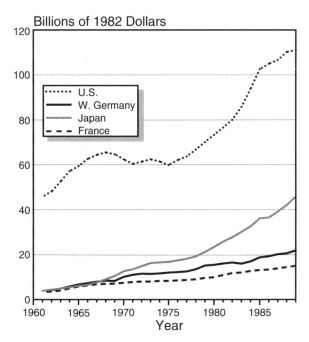

FIGURE 2.1. R&D expenditures in selected advanced industrial economies, 1961–89. (Adapted from National Science Board. 1991. *Science and Engineering Indicators.* Washington, DC: U.S. Government Printing Office.)

1980s, for example, high-technology manufacturing firms were responsible for an average of 58% of all industrial R&D expenditures in the United States (National Science Board 1991). Growth in U.S. R&D expenditures was especially rapid during the 1950s and 1960s. From 1953 to 1960, U.S. R&D expenditures increased on average 15% each year. In contrast to the situation in Japan, West Germany, and elsewhere, much of the R&D expenditure in the United States has been, and remains, defense-related. Most analysts agree, however, that at least through the 1970s, U.S. high-technology firms gained substantial direct and indirect commercial benefit from defense-related R&D. Moreover, the large influence of defense-related R&D notwithstanding, until the 1980s the amount of nondefense-related R&D performed by U.S. firms remained at least double that carried out in Japan.[2]

The U.S. government directly and indirectly underwrote technology development, both through R&D contracts and through military procurement. During the late 1950s, for example, the U.S. government directly sponsored more than 25% of the research performed by U.S. semiconductor firms. Additional government support to those firms was provided through military procurement programs. In 1965 military markets accounted for 28% of total semiconductor production, and for fully 72% of integrated-circuit production, in the United States (Tilton 1971). The high prices paid by the military underwrote much of the risk and costs of new technology development. While the significance of military markets declined during the 1970s, the initial phase of military procurement during the 1960s helped to secure the technological leadership of U.S. firms in the semiconductor industry.

The buildup in science and technology investments in the United States during the middle part of the twentieth century is also evident in the size of the engineering labor force. Training programs at federally funded universities and laboratories provided an increasing supply of engineers and scientists to emergent high-technology industries. Figure 2.2 shows the numbers of scientists and engineers engaged in R&D, relative to the size of the total labor force, in selected countries for the years 1965–1987. In 1965 there were in the United States 64.7 scientists and engineers engaged in R&D for every 10,000 workers. The comparable figures for Japan and West Germany were 24.6 and 22.6, respectively. The number of workers employed in R&D in the United States fell in the early 1970s in both absolute terms and relative to the size of the total labor force,

---

[2]The primary interest here is with the contribution of R&D to the ascendance of U.S. firms in the semiconductor industry through the late 1970s. While total R&D by U.S. firms remains larger than that of all foreign competitors, several negative trends have emerged in the 1980s. The percentage of GNP devoted to R&D is now lower in the United States than in Japan, the former West Germany, and several other advanced industrial economies. During the second half of the 1980s, R&D expenditures in the United States grew at an average annual constant-dollar rate of only 1.2%. Japanese expenditures on nondefense-related R&D in 1989 were close to 60% of U.S. nondefense R&D expenditures, up from 35% in 1970 (National Science Board 1991).

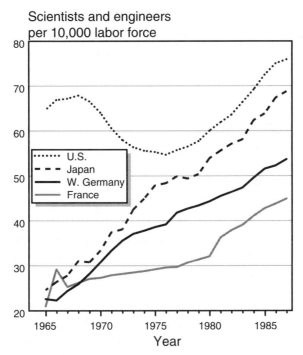

FIGURE 2.2. Scientists and engineers engaged in R&D, selected countries, 1965–87. (Adapted from National Science Board. 1991. *Science and Engineering Indicators.* Washington, DC: U.S. Government Printing Office.)

but R&D employment during that period remained well above the levels achieved in Japan and other industrialized countries. The data in Figure 2.2 also reveal, however, the rapid increase in R&D employment in Japan and West Germany since the early 1970s. Relative to the size of the total labor force in each country, R&D employment in Japan is now close to that in the United States.

Many of the results of basic scientific research (e.g., published research papers) move rapidly into the public domain where they are available to both domestic and foreign firms. During the 1950s and 1960s, domestic firms were the primary beneficiaries of U.S. R&D investments. Large-scale U.S. investments in basic science and engineering translated into market and technology leadership for U.S. firms. This experience contrasts markedly with that of recent years, when Japanese firms and other competitors established effective mechanisms (e.g., by foreign research facilities and investment in U.S. high-technology firms) for the rapid international transfer of technological knowledge. The ability of U.S. firms to "capture" the benefits of investments in science was central to the technological leadership of the United States in the semiconductor industry.

The Organization of Innovation

The emergence of a large science and technology complex in the United States explains much of the initial commercial success of U.S. semiconductor firms. At least since the time of Schumpeter (1934, 1954), however, researchers have insisted that there are important organizational dimensions to innovation and technology development. The return on R&D investment is thought to depend on the organizational and institutional structure of innovation (Cohen and Levin 1989). This has certainly been evident in the U.S. semiconductor industry. From the late 1950s onward, semiconductor manufacturing in the United States evolved within an institutional structure markedly different from that maintained by international competitors.

The organizational structure of the U.S. semiconductor industry is complex, including vertically integrated electronics producers (e.g., Hewlett Packard and IBM), many large and small specialized firms that manufacture semiconductors for open-market or "merchant" sale, and a multitude of independent suppliers and subcontractors. The industry itself is embedded in a broader science infrastructure of universities, research laboratories, consultants, and venture-capital firms. Two elements of this organizational structure stand out as being of central importance. The first is the key role of start-up firms as agents of technological change. The second is the tendency toward an "open" technology environment, that is, toward an accelerated flow of knowledge and information among firms within the U.S. semiconductor industry. These two organizational elements are at the core of the technological dynamism exhibited by the U.S. semiconductor industry. Para-doxically, however, they are now emerging as a source of weak-ness in the changed competitive environment of the 1990s.

New Firm Formation in the U.S. Semiconductor Industry

The lion's share of formal R&D in the semiconductor industry is performed by large established firms, such as AT&T, IBM, and Motorola.[3] These large firms have been responsible for many crucial technological breakthroughs in the industry. During the 1950s, established firms such as G.E. and RCA were the major recipients of government research contracts and were responsible for many key patents on semiconductor technology. The important role of these research laboratories suggested that the semiconductor industry would be highly concentrated, dominated by a few large electronics firms with the resources to carry out basic research in semiconductor technologies. In the case of the U.S. semiconductor industry, however, specialized start-up firms have played a prominent role in the development and deployment of new semiconductor technologies. From Fairchild Semiconductor and Motorola in the 1960s, to Intel, Signetics, and LSI Logic in subsequent decades, specialized merchant firms were responsible for a series of key advances in product and process technologies. The proliferation of start-up firms was unique to the U.S. semiconductor industry; elsewhere, semiconductor manufacturing remained dominated by large, vertically integrated electronics firms.

　　Figure 2.3 shows the number of semiconductor start-up firms by their year-of-entry into the industry for the period 1957–1989. A total of 208 semiconductor firm were founded in the United States during this 32-year period. The formation of new firms has occurred at an uneven rate. Three broad groups of start-ups may be identified, each of which is associated with the application and exploitation of a major technological shift within the semiconductor industry. The first cluster of start-ups appeared during the period 1957–64 and is associated with

---

[3]Much basic theoretical research is, of course, performed in university research laboratories.

Number of firms

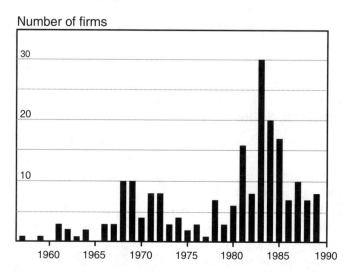

FIGURE 2.3. Semiconductor start-up firms, by year-of-entry, 1957–89.

the initial commercial exploitation of the planar process. The second wave appeared between 1967 and 1973, and includes such successful firms as Intel, National Semiconductor, and Advanced Micro Devices. The majority of firms in this second wave were founded to develop products using Large Scale Integration (LSI) technology, including computer memory and microprocessor devices. The third group, and the largest by far, appeared during the early and mid-1980s and is dominated by firms involved in custom and application-specific device technologies. While numerous factors influenced the timing of the formation of new firms (e.g., changes in tax law that favored venture-capital investments in the early 1980s), these groups are illustrative of the primary role of start-ups as agents for the rapid application and exploitation of new technologies. While the germination of new products and production processes typically took place in the research facilities of large established firms, start-up companies were often at the forefront in developing applications for new technologies.

Why did this pattern of entrepreneurial industrialization emerge in the United States? During much of the first three decades of the industry, barriers-to-entry to semiconductor manufacturing remained relatively low. A large infrastructure of industrial support rapidly emerged to support start-up firms, including specialized venture-capital sources, equipment suppliers, and assembly subcontractors. At the same time, the process of technological change itself undermined learning economies accrued by established firms in the manufacture of existing product lines, creating opportunities for start-up firms. Of greatest significance to the dynamic of new firm-formation and technological development, however, has been the tendency toward a rapid circulation of technological knowl-edge and information among firms in the U.S. semiconductor industry.

The U.S. semiconductor industry is characterized by an open technology-environment in which technological knowl-edge flows relatively rapidly from one firm to another. Histor-ically, two sets of practices have been of particular importance in supporting the diffusion of technology among U.S firms. First, technology diffusion was encouraged by liberal licensing practices established by Bell Laboratories and subsequently adopted by other firms in the industry. Rather than attempting to defend market share through patent litigation, most semi-conductor firms licensed new technologies to other man-ufacturers, providing product and process specifications in re-turn for the payment of royalties on subsequent sales (typically 5–10% of sales).[4] In many cases, licensing was backed by second-source agreements in which firms were licensed as an alternate source of supply for a particular product line; in these cases, the license was typically accompanied by the provision of technical support.[5] Cross-licensing of patented technologies be-came a common practice in the U.S. semiconductor industry.

Of greater practical significance for the diffusion of knowl-

[4]The incidence of patent litigation has increased dramatically during the 1980s, partly in response to a strengthening of intellectual property rights in the 1986 U.S. Semicon-ductor Chip Protection Act. Most patent litigation is eventually settled out of court through licensing agreements.

[5]During the 1960s and 1970s, most major users of semiconductor devices required that suppliers provide multiple sources of supply as insurance against low yields or capacity shortages on the part of the original device manufacturer. Because parts from multiple suppliers must be fully compatible, second-source agreements typically involve a sub-stantial transfer of technological know-how.

edge, however, has been the movement of engineering personnel among firms in the semiconductor industry. From its beginning, the U.S. semiconductor industry has been marked by high levels of interfirm mobility on the part of key engineering and research personnel. Most start-up firms in the industry have been founded by engineers and scientists previously employed by established producers. As workers moved from one firm to another, they carried with them the knowledge and experience crucial to the development and manufacture of semiconductor technologies. While attempts were often made to restrict the outflow of technology, much of the crucial knowledge and information was of a tacit kind and not easily protected by traditional procedures (such as patent law).[6] The rapid diffusion of technological knowledge in the United States gave start-up firms access to requisite skills and information concerning semiconductor products and production processes, and thereby undermined the ability of existing firms to establish oligopolistic control over the industry. Product licensing gave firms the right to manufacture semiconductors; interfirm worker mobility supplied the skills and knowledge necessary to manufacture the devices, thereby alleviating the major barrier-to-entry to the emerging semiconductor industry.

The practice of widespread licensing of semiconductor technologies by U.S. firms was shaped by what Teece (1990) has described as the appropriability conditions surrounding the development and commercial exploitation of technology, that is by the opportunity for firms to capture exclusive returns on R&D investments. Of particular importance is the regulatory environment in the United States, which is characterized by vigorous antitrust enforcement and weak copyright protection standards for intellectual property. In the case of Bell Laboratories, the licensing of semiconductor patents was a direct outgrowth of an anti-trust settlement on the part of AT&T (the

---

[6]As attempts are made to effect some "closure" in the U.S. technology environment, semiconductor firms are experimenting with various strategies to reduce the loss of technology through interfirm worker mobility. For example, several semiconductor producers now have key engineering workers sign agreements stipulating that, upon leaving a firm, they will not develop semiconductors that compete directly with the product lines of their previous employer. The legality of such agreements is currently being contested in the courts.

parent firm). Bell Laboratories actively promoted the transfer of technological knowledge through a series of industry seminars and professional publications.

It is difficult to assess the net effect of this open technology-environment on the U.S. semiconductor industry. Conventional analysis suggests that the "leakage" of technology from one firm to another will lead to an underinvestment in R&D (Arrow 1962).[7] Unable to ensure their exclusive access to the benefits of in-house R&D, firms will tend to reduce internal technology-development efforts. By this account, the technology-development process is enhanced by (a) strong copyright protection of intellectual property, and (b) government intervention (such as government-sponsored basic research) to offset the failure of the market to supply research. On the other hand, the experience of the semiconductor industry suggests that an open technology-environment and the accelerated flow of technology among firms also brings positive benefits. Two processes are of particular significance in this regard.

First, the formation of new firms and the open flow of technology among firms has helped to avoid the "locking-in" of suboptimal technologies. One of the major contributions of start-up firms has been the identification and exploitation of technological pathways and market opportunities not recognized or pursued by established firms. The majority of start-up firms were founded as spin-offs from established producers. Typically, these spin-off ventures were formed to investigate technological opportunities considered too risky by, or unlikely to contribute to the immediate earnings of, the parent firm. Perhaps the classic example of this process is the transition from discrete semiconductor-technology to integrated circuits during the late 1950s. While established electronics firms, such as RCA and Philco, were a major force in the production of discrete devices, it was the new entrants to the industry, such as

---

[7]Neoclassical economic analysis of innovation typically assumes constant returns on investment in R&D and complete transferability of knowledge and information among firms. Over the past decade, however, new lines of analysis have emerged, examining such phenomena as localized knowledge-systems, path dependency, and dynamic economies of scale in R&D. Foray and Freeman (1993) provide a useful introduction to recent work in this area.

Fairchild Semiconductor and Texas Instruments, that pioneered the development of integrated circuits. In an environment of rapid change and technological uncertainty, the actions of start-up firms have served to broaden the scope of
technological activity by allowing the simultaneous pursuit of
multiple technological pathways. Many of these technological
pathways have proven to be dead ends; some have resulted in
key technological and commercial breakthroughs.[8]

Second, the flow of technological information among semiconductor firms has supported a process of collective and
cumulative learning in the industry that has allowed individual
companies to build on the successes and failures of the industry
as a whole. In attempting to solve technological puzzles, semiconductor firms have been able to avoid unnecessary repetition
of research carried out by other firms. In addition to this direct
technological contribution, competition from start-up producers has had a more general effect on the pace of technological
change, forcing established firms continually to seek competitive advantage through new technology-development. The
contribution of start-up firms has thus extended to the creation
of a competitive environment in which profitability depends on
ongoing innovation in products and production processes.

Whether the openness of the U.S. technology environment, and the attendant pattern of entrepreneurial industrialization, has been a net benefit to the technological dynamism of
the U.S. semiconductor industry is unclear and remains an
important area for future research.[9] Recent analysis stresses
the importance of trust and reciprocity to the process of information exchange. In the case of the semiconductor industry, the accelerated circulation of information among firms

[8]The breadth of technological activity has been all the more important given the poor
track record of the defense establishment and other government research-funding
agencies in "picking winners" in semiconductor technology.

[9]The case of microprocessors is instructive in this regard. In the late 1970s, Intel
Corporation broke with previous practice and refused to license the design of the
80386 microprocessor to other firms. Intel reaped enormous profits from the sale of
80386 and 80486 microprocessors, profits that were subsequently ploughed back into
new technology-development. Even as this occurred, an alternative technological path-
way, centered on Reduced Instruction Set Computing (RISC) technology, was being
pioneered by the start-up companies Sun Microsystems and MIPS Technology.

appears to have been accepted only as long as all participants benefitted from the process. A major problem for U.S. firms in this regard has been the one-way flow of technological information from the United States to Japan. Because an open technological environment facilitates the rapid transfer of technological knowledge to foreign competitors, antitrust and copyright issues are at the center of current debates about the competitiveness of the U.S. semiconductor industry in global markets.[10]

The Territoriality of Innovation

Geographers and regional planners have long insisted that there are important locational dimensions in processes of innovation and technology development. In particular, it is often claimed that there is a distinct territoriality to innovation, whereby manufacturing competence becomes embedded within a select number of regions that develop comparative advantage in specific production processes (Malecki 1991). These ideas, however, have only rarely been adopted by nongeographers and have not had a substantial influence on the broader scientific and policy debate concerning competitiveness in high-technology industries.[11]

In the case of the U.S. semiconductor industry, most of the major merchant semiconductor firms are clustered in Silicon Valley, along with many important users of semiconductor devices (the major exceptions are Motorola and Texas Instruments, which are based in Phoenix and Dallas, respectively). This locational concentration of firms in Silicon Valley has been central to the pattern of entrepreneurial innovation and

[10]Support for an open technological environment has been eroded by the widespread perception that the flow of technology has been largely unidirectional, from the United States to Japan, with little reciprocal exchange of knowledge and information. By contrast, while knowledge flows among U.S. semiconductor firms were never neatly balanced, most industry participants acknowledge that information exchange was mutually beneficial for all participants. The tendency in the 1980s was toward a more restricted flow of technology among firms, including the formalization of technological relations through cooperative research contracts. These developments are discussed in detail in Chapters 4 and 5.

[11]See Krugman (1991) and Porter (1990) for recent work that gives recognition to the spatiality of economic processes.

collective learning that emerged in the U.S. semiconductor industry. The close proximity of many specialized manufacturers, suppliers, and users of semiconductor devices in Silicon Valley facilitated communication among firms. At the same time, high levels of interfirm mobility among semiconductor engineers, as well as informal communication among workers, helped to ensure the rapid circulation of new ideas and information within the Silicon Valley production complex.

These locational and territorial dimensions of semiconductor production are examined in the first instance using statistics for SIC 3674 (semiconductors and related devices) drawn from the *Census of Manufactures*. Table 2.1 shows the geographical distribution of domestic semiconductor shipments by census division and for selected states during the period 1958–82. These data indicate that during the 1950s the geographical

TABLE 2.1. Distribution of Shipments (by Value) in SIC 3674 (Semiconductors and Related Devices) for Census Divisions and Selected States, 1958–82

	1958	1963	1967	1972	1977	1982
USA Total	100%	100%	100%	100%	100%	100%
New England	23.4	14.3	n.a.	14.0	n.a.	n.a.
Massachusetts	21.8	8.2	n.a.	n.a.	3.1	2.9
Mid-Atlantic	36.9	37.2	n.a.	30.2	24.3	23.7
New Jersey	9.8	5.4	3.6	1.0	1.0	1.3
New York	15.0	8.8	6.3	18.5	13.6	16.0
Pennsylvania	12.1	23.0	n.a.	10.7	9.7	6.4
East N. Central	n.a.	n.a.	n.a.	n.a.	n.a.	n.a.
West N. Central	n.a.	n.a.	n.a.	n.a.	n.a.	n.a.
South Atlantic	n.a.	n.a.	n.a.	n.a.	n.a.	n.a.
East S. Central	n.a.	n.a.	n.a.	n.a.	n.a.	n.a.
West S. Central	n.a.	n.a.	n.a.	n.a.	n.a.	n.a.
Texas	n.a.	n.a.	n.a.	n.a.	16.0	13.1
Mountain	n.a.	n.a.	n.a.	n.a.	n.a.	n.a.
Arizona	n.a.	n.a.	n.a.	n.a.	8.7	7.4
Pacific	n.a.	n.a.	n.a.	n.a.	n.a.	n.a.
California	13.9	21.8	n.a.	n.a.	34.8	32.7

n.a.: data not available.
Source: U.S. Department of Commerce, Bureau of the Census (1958–82).

location of the semiconductor industry was primarily in the Northeast United States. Fully 58.7% (by value) of U.S. semi-conductor shipments in 1958 originated in Massachusetts and the mid-Atlantic states of New Jersey, New York, and Pennsyl-vania. During the 1960s and 1970s, however, the Sunbelt states of Arizona, California, and Texas replaced the Northeast as the dominant focus of semiconductor production in the United States. The percentage of semiconductor shipments originat-ing in California rose from 13.9% in 1958, to 32.7% in 1982. The declining importance of the Northeast reflected the fail-ure of the old electronics manufacturers in this region to make the transition to the rapidly growing integrated-circuit market.

The rise of Silicon Valley, and the relative decline of semi-conductor production in the Northeast United States, are shown graphically in Figure 2.4 using data drawn from *County Business Patterns*. The percentage of U.S. employment in SIC 3674 firms concentrated in Silicon Valley (Santa Clara County) increased from 11% in 1964, to a peak of 29% in 1982. By the mid-1970s, the region had emerged as the new organizational and geographical hub of the semiconductor industry. In con-trast to Dallas, Phoenix, and other centers of merchant semi-conductor manufacturing in the United States, Silicon Valley developed by way of a highly entrepreneurial mode of in-dustrialization, involving large numbers of start-up firms and a tendency toward the vertical and horizontal disintegration of production. The cluster of start-up firms in Silicon Valley was at the center of the technological dynamism and rapid growth of the U.S. semiconductor industry through the 1970s.

The Growth of Silicon Valley

The foundations of a semiconductor industry in Silicon Valley were laid in the late 1950s by Shockley Laboratories, Fairchild Semiconductor, and Rheem. These semiconductor firms, in conjunction with a small number of electronics manufacturers (especially Hewlett Packard, Lockheed, and Varian), formed the initial base for the huge high-technology complex that was to emerge in the region during the next two decades.

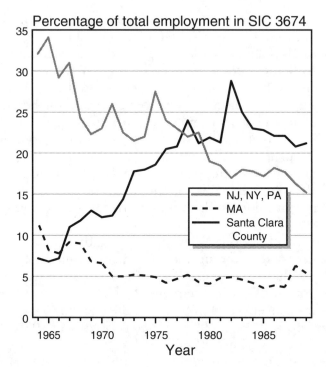

FIGURE 2.4. Percentage of semiconductor industry employment in the United States, the Northeast, and Santa Clara County, 1964–89. (Adapted from U.S. Department of Commerce, Bureau of the Census. 1964–89. *County Business Patterns.* Washington, DC: U.S. Government Printing Office.)

Table 2.2 shows total employment and number of establishments in SIC 3674 (semiconductors and related devices) for Santa Clara County (Silicon Valley) during the period 1964–89. These data reveal that semiconductor production in Silicon Valley expanded at only a moderate pace through the mid-1960s. Fairchild Semiconductor, with some 3,500 workers, was at this time by far the largest semiconductor employer in the region. Much of the employment growth in Silicon Valley during the early 1960s was generated not by semiconductor producers, but by the rapidly expanding aerospace and electronics activities of the Lockheed Corporation (centered on Moffett Field Naval Air Station in Mountain View, California).

TABLE 2.2. Employment and Number of Establishments in SIC 3674, Santa Clara County, 1964–89

Year	Total employment	Number of establishments
1964	3,994	7
1965	4,164	8
1966	6,042	9
1967	8,377	8
1968	10,095	8
1969	12,338	15
1970	12,290	26
1971	9,684	28
1972	11,491	35
1973	16,388	36
1974	24,432	49
1975	18,786	53
1976	21,779	63
1977	24,988	65
1978	29,578	67
1979	28,810	91
1980	34,453	92
1981	34,775	108
1982	50,998	135
1983	39,589	127
1984	43,661	134
1985	47,069	136
1986	40,424	124
1987	39,857	133
1988	37,563	128
1989	39,945	124

Source: U.S. Department of Commerce, Bureau of the Census (1964–89).

The Missile and Space division of Lockheed, located in Mountain View, grew from a handful of employees in the mid-1950s, to more than 23,000 in 1963 (Stewart 1967). From the late 1960s onward, however, the commercial success of such Silicon Valley firms as Fairchild Semiconductor, Intel, National Semiconductor, Signetics, and a host of other smaller merchant producers supported a major increase in employment in the region. Employment in SIC 3674 in Silicon Valley increased from less than 6,000 in the early 1960s, to 34,453 in 1980.

Most of the semiconductor firms located in Silicon Valley were founded as "spin-offs" from existing semiconductor producers. Table 2.3 lists all of the firms founded in Santa Clara County by year-of-entry into the semiconductor industry during the period 1955–76. All of the semiconductor operations established during the 1960s, with the exception of Siliconix and Stewart-Warner, were founded by, or staffed with, key

TABLE 2.3. Semiconductor Firms Founded in Santa Clara County, 1955–76

Year	Semiconductor firms
1955	Shockley Laboratories[a]
1957	Fairchild Semiconductor[a]
1959	Rheem[a]
1961	Amelco (Teledyne), Hewlett Packard, Signetics
1962	Molectro[a], Siliconix
1963	General Micro-Electronics[a]
1964	Stewart-Warner[a], Union Carbide[a]
1966	American Microsystems[a], Cal-Dak[a]
1967	Electronic Arrays[a], Intersil, Microwave Associates[a], National Semiconductor,
1968	Advanced Memory Systems[a], Avantek, Cermetek, Integrated Systems Technology[a], Intel, Kinetic Technology[a], Nortec[a], Qualidyne[a]
1969	Advanced Micro Devices, Cartesian[a], Communications Transistor, Four Phase Systems, Intech, Lithic Systems[a], Precision Monoliths
1970	Advanced LSI, Integrated Electronics[a], International Computer Modules[a], Litronix[a], Monolithic Memories, Signetics Memory[a], Varadyne[a]
1971	Antex[a], Cal-Tex[a], Exar, EG&G Reticon, Intersil Memory[a], Micro Power, Standard Microsystems[a]
1972	IC Transducers[a], Interdesign[a], International Micro-Circuits, LSI Systems[a], Optical Diodes[a], Opto-Ray[a]
1973	Advanced Memory Systems, Data General, Synertek[a]
1974	Monosil[a], Zilog
1975	Maruman Integrated Circuits[a], Mneumonics[a], Semi-Processes
1976	Cognition[a], Supertex

[a]Firm now closed or acquired by another producer.
Sources: Compiled from data in Hoefler (1968), *Fortune Product Directory* (1959), Tilton (1971), and company reports.

engineering personnel who had at some time worked at Fairchild Semiconductor (Hoefler 1971). Thus, in the early 1960s, Amelco, Signetics, General Micro-Electronics, and Molectro were founded by ex-Fairchild employees. These firms in turn gave birth to Advanced Micro Devices, Intersil, Intel, National Semiconductor, and others. Hoefler (1968) named this emerging complex of specialized semiconductor firms in Santa Clara County "Silicon Valley."

The spin-off phenomenon was *not* restricted to Fairchild Semiconductor and Silicon Valley. For example, Motorola produced three spin-off semiconductor companies in the mid-1960s, each of which chose to locate close to the parent company in Arizona. The three firms were Dickson Electronics (located in Scottsdale), General Semiconductor (located in Tempe), and Integrated Circuit Engineering (located in Phoenix). Other examples of spin-offs that were created in the 1960s include American Power Devices (from Transitron), Microwave Semiconductor (from RCA), and Mostek (from Texas Instruments). In most cases these spin-off companies operated in the same broad product markets as the "parent" firms. The spin-offs from Motorola were, like the "parent" firm, primarily engaged in production of discrete devices.

What distinguishes the Fairchild Semiconductor-Silicon Valley process is both the number and the commercial success (especially in the area of integrated circuits) of the many firms that trace their bloodlines back to Fairchild Semiconductor. The initial wave of successful spin-offs from Fairchild Semiconductor seems to have been the result of (a) dissatisfaction with the priority accorded to the semiconductor division by the parent company (Fairchild Camera and Instrument), and (b) Fairchild's position among U.S. producers as the firm with the most technologically advanced product line. Fairchild Semiconductor was founded in 1957 as a division of the New Jersey-based Fairchild Camera and Instrument. The semiconductor division initially generated large profits as sales boomed from $500 thousand in 1958, to $140 million in 1967. However, much of the profit from the sales of semiconductors was fed into other, less successful divisions of the parent company rather than reinvested in new product and process technologies (Braun and MacDonald 1982). Press reports of the time describe employees leaving Fairchild in frustration at the organizational structure and financial policies of the parent company (Hoefler 1968). For example, in 1967 alone, close to forty members of Fairchild's managerial and engineering staff (including General Manager Charles Sporck) left the company and joined Silicon Valley start-up National Semiconductor.

Whatever the precise reasons for the initial wave of spin-offs, the important issue for present purposes is the subsequent commercial success of the many new semiconductor firms founded in Silicon Valley. Merchant semiconductor firms such as National Semiconductor and Signetics in the 1960s, and more recently Intel and LSI Logic, were responsible for many of the major technological breakthroughs achieved in the industry and were at the forefront in the identification and development of new markets for semiconductor devices. As the number of suppliers, customers, and subcontractors in Silicon Valley increased during the 1960s and 1970s, semiconductor firms were able to secure substantial economies of agglomeration in their manufacturing operations.

Economies of Agglomeration in Silicon Valley

The advantages of locating in Silicon Valley took two basic forms, namely, enhanced access to, and communication with, customers and suppliers, and efficiencies in hiring and recruitment within the local labor market. Research by Scott and Angel (1987) shows that semiconductor producers in Silicon Valley are distinguished from other U.S. semiconductor firms by the high percentage of shipments made to customers located within the production complex. Of particular importance in this regard has been the emergence of Silicon Valley as a major center for the computer and communications industries. In addition, location in Silicon Valley provided semiconductor firms with local access to key equipment and materials suppliers.

The scale and significance of these economies of agglomeration are difficult to measure. Recent research by Angel (1993), Gordon (1992), and Saxenian (1991), among others, suggests that local access to customers and suppliers is especially important at the product-development stage of the manufacturing process. At this stage, product design is accelerated by frequent communication among the engineering and research staffs of customers and suppliers. By contrast, proximity is of less significance in the actual production of high-technology systems because most manufacturers use components produced by a global network of suppliers.

Local access to customers and suppliers appears to be of greatest importance for small start-up firms that lack the global manufacturing and marketing capabilities of established producers. Recent research (Schoonhoven, Eisenhardt, and Lyman 1990; Eisenhardt and Schoonhoven 1990) suggests that Silicon Valley has served as an important incubator for start-up semiconductor firms. Start-up firms founded in Silicon Valley ship their first product for revenue faster than other new ventures. On average, three years after their founding, Silicon Valley start-up firms have created twice as many new jobs as have semiconductor firms founded in any other region of the United States, and the former have sales valued at three times those of the latter.

In addition to these local linkage-effects, the clustering of semiconductor firms in Silicon Valley has allowed the realization of significant economies of agglomeration in labor-market processes. Earlier studies by Angel (1989, 1990) demonstrate that fluid employment relations and efficiencies in search and mobility within the local labor market allow Silicon Valley firms remarkable flexibility in meeting their labor demands. The close proximity of semiconductor producers in Silicon Valley facilitates the types of interfirm worker mobility and information exchange that are central to the entrepreneurial industrialization in the region. Analysis of work-history data reveals that even after controlling for differences in industrial structure (such as size of firm), semiconductor engineers in Silicon Valley have a higher level of interfirm worker mobility than do engineers employed elsewhere in the United States

(Angel 1989). One consequence of this interfirm mobility is that firms in Silicon Valley have the opportunity to recruit workers with experience from the local labor market, thereby avoiding the need to develop requisite skills and experience in-house (e.g., through internal training programs).

Table 2.4 shows the hiring patterns in 1986 for a sample of semiconductor establishments located in Silicon Valley and elsewhere in the United States. Data are provided on the percentage of workers hired with experience, and on the amount of prior work experience (in years) required of new hires. Information is provided for three occupations, namely, fabrication-line operative, process technician, and process engineer. In all three occupations, Silicon Valley semiconductor firms tend to fill a high proportion of job vacancies with workers possessing prior work experience. In the case of production engineers, for example, Silicon Valley firms filled 93% of job vacancies by hiring experienced workers.

TABLE 2.4. Hiring Patterns of Semiconductor Establishments, by Location, 1986

	Silicon Valley	Not Silicon Valley	
		>10 plants	<10 plants[a]
Experience required (years)			
Fabrication workers[b]	0.9	0.2	0.1
Technicians[b]	1.8	1.0	0.6
Engineers	1.3	1.1	0.9
Percentage hired with experience			
Fabrication workers[b]	78.5	52.6	48.7
Technicians[b]	90.5	73.3	70.4
Engineers	93.0	88.7	70.6
Number of plants in sample	24	14	29

[a]Locations outside of Silicon Valley with more than, or less than, 10 semiconductor establishments.
[b]F-test indicates that group means are significantly different at the 0.05 level of confidence.
Source: Angel (1991). Copyright 1991 Pion Limited, London.

Table 2.5 provides parallel information on the geography of hiring by semiconductor firms. Semiconductor firms fill the majority of job vacancies from within the local labor market, drawing on the large pool of specialized labor skills within their region. Among semiconductor establishments located elsewhere in the United States, there are significant differences across occupations in the tendency toward local hiring. In the case of fabrication-line operatives, the vast majority of job vacancies are filled from within the local labor market. In technical and engineering occupations, by contrast, a substantial number of vacancies are filled from outside the local labor market. In the case of process engineers, Silicon Valley firms fill a total of 85.4% of job vacancies from the local labor market, compared with 54.1% and 33.2% for firms located elsewhere in the United States. The ability to fill job vacancies by hiring experienced workers from the local labor market is one of the major advantages attracting start-up semiconductor firms to Silicon Valley.

As with many other aspects of this dense production conplex, the dynamic of interfirm worker mobility has its costs; in this case, semiconductor firms in Silicon Valley incur sub-

TABLE 2.5. The Geography of Hiring by Semiconductor Establishments, by Location, 1986

	Silicon Valley	Not Silicon Valley	
		>10 plants	<10 plants[a]
Percentage hired locally			
Fabrication workers[b]	100.0	100.0	98.6
Technicians[b]	87.1	81.2	68.2
Engineers[b]	85.4	54.1	33.2
Number of plants in sample	24	14	29

[a]Locations outside of Silicon Valley with more than, or less than, 10 semiconductor establishments.
[b]*F*-test indicates that group means are significantly different at the 0.05 level of confidence.
Source: Angel (1991). Copyright 1991 Pion Limited, London.

stantial disadvantage through the loss of experienced workers to competing producers. For most Silicon Valley start-up firms, however, the benefits of participation in this local labor market, and above all the ability to hire key engineering personnel from the external local labor market, far outweigh the costs. Lacking extensive in-house training programs, start-firms in Silicon Valley are able rapidly to assemble research teams by hiring skilled and experienced engineers from the external labor market.

Semiconductor firms in Silicon Valley have also benefitted from the influx of immigrant labor to the region, a dynamic that has helped to alleviate upward pressure on wages in low-skilled production jobs. Table 2.6 shows the composition of the production work force in 1986 for a sample of semiconductor establishments located in Silicon Valley and elsewhere in the United States. Silicon Valley establishments are distinguished by the high percentage of Asian and Hispanic production

TABLE 2.6. Composition of the Semiconductor Production Work Force, 1986

	Silicon Valley	Not Silicon Valley	
		>10 plants	<10 plants[a]
By gender (%)			
Female	64.6	76.2	72.4
By race/ethnicity (%)			
Asian[b]	38.3	28.6	7.2
Black	4.3	5.8	9.4
Hispanic[b]	17.0	14.5	8.9
White[b]	37.4	50.2	71.4
Other	2.7	0.9	3.1
Number of plants in sample	24	14	29

[a]Locations outside of Silicon Valley with more than, or less than, 10 semiconductor establishments.
[b]F-test indicates that group means are significantly different at the 0.05 level of confidence.
Source: Angel (1991). Copyright 1991 Pion Limited, London.

workers. As described in detail by Siegel and Borock (1982) and Snow (1983), during the 1960s and 1970s Asian and Hispanic women replaced white women as the predominant production workers in Silicon Valley.

The forms of entrepreneurial industrialization and accelerated information flow characteristic of the U.S. semiconductor industry have, in sum, a marked territorial dimension. While Silicon Valley is only one part of an industry that also comprises large producers located elsewhere in the United States, the region has been, and remains, the technological hub of semiconductor manufacturing in the United States. The globalization of semiconductor manufacturing notwithstanding, the majority of U.S. and foreign semiconductor firms maintain R&D facilities in Silicon Valley in an apparent attempt to tap into the large pool of labor skills and forms of technological learning sustained within the region.

PRODUCTION UNDER CONDITIONS OF RAPID TECHNOLOGICAL CHANGE

Innovation and technological development are at the core of the rapid growth and commercial domination sustained by U.S. semiconductor firms through the late 1970s. It is this aspect of semiconductor manufacturing that has captured the attention of both manufacturers and most industry observers alike. In the vocabulary of the industry, U.S. semiconductor manufacturers are "technology driven," focusing their best resources and expertise on the development of new technologies. The manufacturing forms that emerged in the U.S. semiconductor industry, from start-up producers to the research laboratories of large firms, were in practice extremely conducive to the rapid development and deployment of new technologies.

U.S. semiconductor firms have been less successful, however, in addressing problems within the domain of production. Throughout the 1960s and 1970s, U.S. semiconductor firms encountered persistent problems of production quality and fluctuating capacity utilization, as well as difficulties in achieving adequate rates of return on investments. The source of these problems lay in an overly narrow conception of technological change, and in a tendency to uncritically adopt manufacturing practices from other industrial sectors, such as automobiles and steel.

With the emergence of mass markets for integrated circuits beginning in the mid-1960s, issues relating to production became increasingly important to the profitability of U.S. semiconductor firms. In meeting the rapidly growing demand of industrial and consumer markets, U.S. semiconductor firms for the most part adopted a classic sequential model of manufacturing, which broke down the manufacturing process into a linear chain of discrete stages (basic research, product development, production, marketing, and so forth). Within this disassembled manufacturing form, each stage in the process was viewed as a separate manufacturing task employing different kinds of workers and involving different manufacturing imperatives. In the case of the U.S. semiconductor industry, a kind of bifurcated manufacturing system emerged. One segment, comprising research and product development, was oriented toward technology development and problems of innovation; the other segment, comprising production and assembly operations, was driven by issues of production cost. Issues of innovation and technological change stopped at the door of product development; production facilities were optimized to minimize costs.

In general, the drive to lower production costs centered on two key strategies. The first involved the exploitation of product-specific economies of scale. Semiconductor manufacturers typically achieve poor yields on the initial production runs of new devices. With increasing production volumes, yields and unit costs improve as firms fine-tune the production process and eliminate sources of device failure (the so-called learning curve effect). As a result, the lowest-cost producers are typically firms with high total production volumes. In order to achieve low unit costs, manufacturers construct high-volume production facilities dedicated to particular product lines. Within these production facilities, semiconductor manufacturers seek to establish a stabile and routine production procedure that minimizes product and process variation in an effort to preserve a high-yield production process.

Routinization of production was accompanied by a search for lower total-factor input costs in production. To this end, U.S. semiconductor manufacturers rapidly adopted a classic tripartite spatial and international division of labor comprising (a) centers of innovation and product development located within major high-technology complexes, (b) routinized high-volume fabrication facilities located at dispersed low-wage sites outside of major metropolitan areas in the United States, and (c) labor-intensive assembly operations at low-wage locations offshore. The dispersal of production and assembly functions was initiated early in the 1960s. The first merchant semiconductor branch plants were opened by Fairchild Semiconductor in South Portland, Maine, and on an Indian reservation in Shiprock, New Mexico. The following year, Motorola, Texas Instruments, and Signetics each opened branch plants in the United States (in Mesa, Arizona, Sherman, Texas, and Orem, Utah, respectively). In the course of the next two decades, all of the major U.S. merchant semiconductor firms followed suit.

Locational dispersal of routinized assembly activities was in part a response to rising land and labor costs, and to occasional labor shortages in Silicon Valley and the other major metropolitan locations for semiconductor production in the United States. In addition, semiconductor producers in Silicon Valley faced a problem of labor turnover among experienced production workers. Most of the major semiconductor manufacturers in Silicon Valley (especially Fairchild Semiconductor, National Semiconductor, and Signetics) secured their operative work forces by recruiting inexperienced workers who were then provided with in-house training. However, once assembly workers had gained training and experience in one of these large firms, they were often lured away by offers of higher wages at smaller firms (1972). A steady stream of experienced production workers flowed from large to small semiconductor firms in Silicon Valley. Large merchant producers sought to reduce their labor turnover, and eliminate this drain of experienced production workers, by locating routinized production activities at various isolated branch locations. For example, Signetics reported that in the late 1960s the turnover rate at its new branch plant in Utah was approximately one third of that sustained at its Silicon Valley assembly facility (Hoefler 1968). In the course of the next three decades, all of the major semiconductor manufacturers set up production and assembly branch plants in the United States and offshore.

The dispersal of fabrication facilities in the United States has been paralleled by the relocation of assembly activities to low-wage sites in selected parts of the world semiperiphery. While several firms carry out assembly operations in the United States (e.g., IBM), the vast majority of assembly work is performed in Southeast Asia. Figure 2.5 shows the locations of U.S.-owned assembly branch plants in 1988, as identified by Scott and Angel (1988). The first such offshore assembly plant was established in 1961 by Fairchild Semiconductor in Hong Kong. During the 1960s, Fairchild, General Instrument, Motorola, Philco-Ford, RCA, Signetics, Texas Instruments, and TRW added offshore assembly plants in Hong Kong, Korea, Mexico, Singapore, and Taiwan. More recently, assembly branch plants have been opened in Indonesia and Thailand.

With the consolidation of this emergent spatial and international division of labor in production, semiconductor manufacturing assumed an organizational and geographical form similar to that of many other industrial sectors, such as automobiles, consumer appliances, and textiles. Indeed, it is clear that the production strategies adopted by U.S. semiconductor firms borrowed heavily from the best practice in other sectors of mass production, in terms of both the development of dedicated production lines and the search for low-cost production locations.

In the case of the semiconductor industry, however, rapid technological change created serious difficulties in the area of production, exposing a fundamental tension between the pressure to develop new technologies, on one hand, and the strategies used to minimize productions costs on existing products, on the other hand. Production problems took two principal forms, namely, fluctuating capacity utilization and low yields.

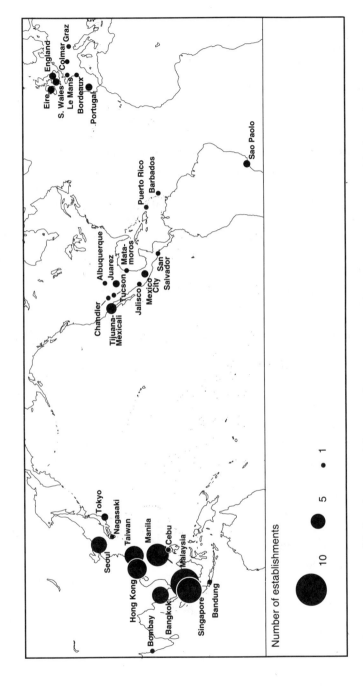

FIGURE 2.5. World distribution of free-standing U.S.-owned semiconductor assembly branch plants. (From Scott and Angel 1988. Copyright 1988 Pion Limited, London.)

The production strategies adopted by U.S. semiconductor firms involved significant up-front investment in dedicated production facilities. When the product lines of a particular firm were successful, high levels of capacity utilization were achieved and the firm was able to drive down production costs and capture a large market share. Conversely, poor market acceptance led to substantial idle capacity. To a certain degree, this problem was offset by second source agreements among semiconductor firms. Throughout the 1960s and 1970s, however, U.S. semiconductor firms were plagued by the problem of matching available production capacity to product demand. This problem was exacerbated by rapid developments in process technologies that required semiconductor firms to regularly update their manufacturing facilities, and by fluctuating market demand for semiconductors.[12]

Low production yields have been a persistent problem for U.S. semiconductor firms. During early production runs, production yields of below 20% were not uncommon on new devices. While yields improved considerably as production volume increased, failure rates remained substantial, requiring extensive and expensive testing of finished products. For much of the 1960s and 1970s, low yields were regarded as an inevitable feature of semiconductor production. It is now becoming increasingly clear, however, that these problems were at least in part a result of the production strategies adopted by U.S. firms. Specifically, the organizational and geographical separation of technology development and production generated serious problems of "manufacturability," as the design of new devices proceeded with insufficient input from production engineers concerning the possibility of achieving high yields on different product technologies.

At the root of the production difficulties experienced by U.S. firms was a tendency to view rapid technological change as

---

[12]During the past three decades, demand for semiconductors has gone through a series of boom and bust cycles. Production capacity utilization for the U.S. semiconductor industry as a whole has varied from 90% to less than 50%. Uncertainty concerning market demand has often been compounded by a tendency on the part of some customers to "double-book" the same order with several different semiconductor firms as a hedge against supply shortages.

almost exclusively a problem of innovation (i.e., how to develop the next generation of technology); the actual production of semiconductor devices was carried out with little regard to the pattern of rapid technological change that characterized the industry. In a complex and constantly changing technological environment, the organizational and geographical separation of technology development and production undermined the ability of firms to codevelop both new products and new production capability. Moreover, the use of dedicated production lines to achieve lower production costs was in fundamental conflict with the highly uncertain and constantly changing environment of product- and process-technology development.

Throughout much of the 1960s and 1970s, U.S. firms experienced high levels of instability in production. Market share and manufacturing demands varied widely from year to year as rival firms introduced new product and process technologies. While severely impacting semiconductor firms, the costs of this instability were also passed on to equipment and materials suppliers in the form of highly uncertain demand, thereby undermining the ability of suppliers to finance the development of next-generation manufacturing technologies. As long as the United States retained its technological advantage over international rivals, these competitive difficulties primarily affected the profit margins of semiconductor firms rather than the position of dominance of those firms in world markets. With the rapid development of Japanese semiconductor firms, however, the weaknesses of U.S. firms were quickly exposed.

SUMMARY

The foundations for the technological dynamism and rapid growth experienced by the U.S. semiconductor industry are very complex. This chapter has highlighted many of the distinctive features of high-technology manufacturing in the United States that have contributed to the pattern of rapid technological change in semiconductors, including the extensive infrastructure of basic research institutions, the open technological environment, and the complex pattern of entrepreneurial industrialization associated with new firm-formation in Silicon Valley and elsewhere. The technological dynamism of Silicon Valley has rested on the rapid circulation of ideas and information within the production complex, and on the ability of start-up firms to rapidly develop and deploy emerging technologies. The activities of start-up firms have never been self-sustaining, however; the technology development activities of start-up firms have always depended on a broader infrastructure of research and product development within established firms and public research laboratories.

Two issues require further emphasis at this time. First, many aspects of the organizational structure of the U.S. semiconductor industry that were a source of strength and dynamism throughout the 1970s are now emerging as a source of weakness under the changed conditions of global competition in the 1990s. In particular, the tendency toward an open technology-environment, and the dependence on start-up firms as key agents of technological change, have facilitated a largely one-way flow of technological information from the United States to foreign competitors. Second, the manufacturing forms that emerged during the period of rapid growth and technological development contained within them structural weaknesses, above all in the area of production, that created the crucial point-of-entry for foreign competition. Loss of market share during the 1980s was a result not only of changes in external competition, but also of a failure on the part of U.S. semiconductor firms to address fully the challenges of production under conditions of rapid technological change.

CHAPTER 3

The Challenge of Global Competition

From the mid-1970s onward, the terms of competition and the structure of manufacturing systems in the semiconductor industry began to change dramatically. Industrial restructuring was driven by two key intersecting processes. The first involved the erosion of U.S. technological and market leadership and the emergence of advanced semiconductor-manufacturing capability in Japan, South Korea, and several Western European countries. The second involved a rapid expansion of non-U.S. markets for semiconductor products. These two intertwined dimensions of economic globalization triggered far-reaching changes in the organization and geography of the U.S. semiconductor industry. They also stimulated widespread debate about the durability of the manufacturing forms that characterized semiconductor production in the United States.

My analysis of these developments begins with the challenge from Japan. The rise to market dominance of Japan during the 1980s confounded the predictions of much of the established economic development theory, which emphasizes the cumulative and self-reinforcing character of competitive advantage in advanced technological development. By this account, the early leaders in new technologies are able to draw on their accrued knowledge and experience to extend their manufacturing advantage over time. In addition, established manufacturing centers often realize important economies of scale in production (either internally, within a firm, or externally, within a regional production complex) that act as a significant barrier-to-entry for new competitors. While knowledge and information eventually diffuse broadly within the global economy (the so-called spread effect), new competitors face significant difficulties in catching up to industry leaders.[1]

In the case of the semiconductor industry, several features of the manufacturing process would tend to support the continued dominance of U.S. firms. First, much technological knowledge and manufacturing capability is generated through a process of learning-by-doing; experience gained from the production of existing devices provides the basis for the manufacture of next-generation products. U.S. market dominance in leading-edge devices effectively excluded foreign competitors from a key arena of learning within the semiconductor industry. Second, the economies of scale and scope realized by the U.S. semiconductor industry created substantial barriers-to-entry in the area of advanced semiconductor manufacturing. Of particular importance in this regard are the synergies that were achieved between U.S. semiconductor firms and local customers and suppliers. Throughout the 1970s, the United States was both the dominant market for advanced semiconductor devices and the major supplier of advanced semiconductor manufacturing equipment. Established linkages and information flows with customers and suppliers were a major source of advantage for U.S. semiconductor firms.

These competitive advantages notwithstanding, U.S. semiconductor firms rapidly lost market share to Japanese firms during the 1980s. With help from the Japanese government, and on the back of a protected domestic market, Japanese semiconductor firms were able to catch up with the United States in key areas of process and equipment technology. Once a technologically sophisticated semiconductor industry was established in Japan, weaknesses in U.S. manufacturing practices

[1]When new industrial centers rise to the fore, it is often on the basis of a major shift in the technological paradigm that undermines accrued competitive advantage (as apparently occurred with the emergence of the integrated-circuit industry in Silicon Valley). Changing technological pathways create a window of opportunity for a geographical shift in centers of manufacturing competence (see Storper and Walker 1989).

were rapidly exposed. The challenge to U.S. dominance emerged first in the area of production, where U.S. firms faced the persistent problems of process control, low production yields, and fluctuating capacity utilization. Subsequently, U.S. firms faced a severe erosion of their leadership in many key areas of product and process technology. The consequences of the Japanese challenge for the U.S. semiconductor industry were, however, far from straightforward. The intensification of U.S.–Japanese competition coincided with a period of profound change in semiconductor product and process technologies, and with a substantial shift in the balance of economies of scope and scale within the industry. While Japanese firms gained substantial market share in computer memories, U.S. firms remained dominant in many other highly profitable market segments. Indeed, part of the explanation for the rapid growth in Japanese market share during the early 1980s is that U.S. firms tended to redeploy production capacity into the manufacture of microprocessors and other design-intensive product lines.

U.S.–JAPANESE COMPETITION IN SEMICONDUCTORS

During the 1980s, the U.S. share of worldwide open-market semiconductor sales fell from 58% to 37%; during the same period, Japanese firms increased their market share from 26% to 49%. The loss of U.S. market share was made all the more dramatic by the fact that Japanese gains occurred not in older, routinized technologies (such as transistors and other discrete semiconductor devices), but in leading-edge high-volume markets. By the mid-1980s, Japan had surpassed the United States as the largest producer of semiconductors worldwide. In many areas of process technology and manufacturing performance, Japanese firms are now the acknowledged world leaders.

How did this dramatic advance in the Japanese semiconductor industry come about? The popular view, widely promoted by U.S. semiconductor firms through the Semiconductor Industry Association and other industry groups, is that

Japan's success rests on a combination of (a) government research subsidies; (b) a protected domestic market; and (c) dumping of semiconductors at below fair-market-value in the United States. Through market protection, investment, and industrial policy, the Japanese government intervened strategically in the market, overcoming the technological leadership of U.S. firms and shifting competitive advantage decisively away from the United States to Japan. In the face of "unfair" competition from Japan, U.S. firms were unable to remain profitable and withdrew from key product markets.[2]

While there is much of value in this account, it provides only a partial understanding of the competitive success of Japanese firms. In particular, it tends to overemphasize the role of the Japanese government, and especially the Japanese Ministry of International Trade and Industry (MITI), and to underestimate the significance of structural weaknesses in the U.S. semiconductor industry. During the mid-1970s, MITI sponsored a series of research programs to establish domestic competence in Very Large Scale Integration (VLSI) integrated-circuit production (Johnson, 1985). Initial efforts focused on the development of advanced capability in manufacturing equipment and process technology. The MITI-sponsored cooperative research effort played a key role in allowing Japanese semiconductor firms to catch up to the United States in process technology during the late 1970s. The subsequent competitive success of Japanese firms, however, had less to do with this much publicized form of government intervention than with the internal development efforts of individual firms and the superior manufacturing performance achieved by Japanese semiconductor producers throughout much of the 1980s.

---

[2]Just what constitutes "fair" competition is far from clear. Japanese firms have clearly maintained a different development strategy from that of the United States, including greater involvement of the government, close partnership relations between customers and suppliers, and strategic pricing to maximize long-term market share. Of greatest concern to U.S. firms have been difficulties experienced in securing sales in Japanese markets. To the extent that poor sales in Japan by U.S. firms reflect a Japanese policy to purchase from domestic suppliers (even if products of superior quality or lower price are available from U.S. firms), U.S. semiconductor manufacturers have a legitimate basis on which to call for U.S. government intervention. Resolution to this problem is likely to require negotiated changes in the trading relationship between the United States and Japan, either through a bilateral agreement, or through the ongoing multilateral GATT trade talks.

The sources of Japan's competitive advantage are seen most clearly in the manufacture of DRAM (dynamic random access memory) integrated circuits.

Japanese Competition in DRAMs

The Japanese development effort initially focused on high-volume production of dynamic random access memory circuits. DRAMs and other memory devices constitute an important segment of the semiconductor market because they are a key component of most electronic systems, from computers to pocket calculators. Worldwide sales of DRAM devices in 1990 totalled $6.6 billion, or approximately 16% (by value) of all integrated-circuit sales. The significance of DRAMs extends beyond the scale of the market, however, these devices have been, and remain, the principal process-technology "driver" in the semiconductor industry. Improvements in manufacturing tolerances, higher circuit densities, and other advances in process technologies typically are achieved first in DRAM products and subsequently diffuse throughout the remainder of the industry. Because DRAMs typically involve a repetitive circuit design and long production runs, they are a good vehicle for stabilizing and perfecting process technology, manufacturing equipment, and chemical performance.[3]

Figure 3.1 shows the shares of the worldwide market (DRAM and other allied products) for selected countries during the period 1978–91.[4] The first DRAM integrated-circuit products (1K DRAM) were manufactured in 1970 by the U.S.

[3]There is currently much speculation among semiconductor manufacturers about the likely continuation of DRAMs as the unchallenged process-technology driver for the industry. In recent years the process-technology gap between DRAMs and advanced logic devices (e.g., microprocessors) has substantially narrowed. In 1992, the U.S. firm LSI Logic announced the development of an industry-leading 0.65 micron fabrication process for high-density gate-array production. Note also that while improvements in process technologies and high-volume automated production have been driven by the DRAM commodity market, advances in other key areas of manufacturing, such as circuit design, testing, materials flow management, packaging, and architecture simulation have been more closely associated with gate arrays and other design-intensive products.

[4]In addition to DRAMs, several other types of memories are manufactured, including Static Random Access Memory (SRAM), Electronically Erasable Programmable Read Only Memory (EEPROM), and Read Only Memory (ROM) devices. DRAMs currently make up approximately 50% of the total market for memory devices.

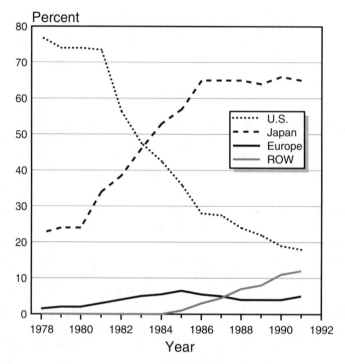

FIGURE 3.1. Percentage shares of worldwide memory market, by country, 1978–91.

firm Intel. During the next decade, a series of evermore complex DRAM devices were introduced (4K DRAMs in 1975, 16K DRAMs in 1977, 64K DRAMs in 1980), pushing forward the frontier of miniaturization in the semiconductor industry. Through the mid-1970s, Japanese firms lagged behind U.S. producers in key areas of process technology and had no significant share of the U.S. market for leading-edge devices. By the late 1970s, however, Japanese firms began to ship substantial volumes of DRAM devices to the United States, and subsequently gained a large share of the U.S. market. In a dramatic turnaround, Japan surpassed the United States in 1983 as the largest merchant producer of memory devices in the world. By 1991, Japanese companies held 65% of a worldwide memory market totalling in excess of $13 billion. In the case of DRAM devices, Japan's share was even higher, amounting to 70% of open-market sales (Integrated Circuit Engineering Corporation [ICE] 1992).

Achieving Parity with U.S. Firms

What was the basis for Japan's rapid rise to dominance in DRAM markets? The initial obstacle for Japanese firms was achieving parity with the United States in key areas of process technology and semiconductor manufacturing equipment. Lacking a strong domestic equipment industry, Japanese producers were dependent on manufacturing equipment supplied by U.S. firms. By the time Japanese firms acquired manufacturing equipment and stabilized it on the production-line, U.S. firms had already begun production with the next generation of technology.

In the mid-1970s, MITI organized a collaborative research effort to bring Japanese semiconductor firms up to parity with U.S. firms in VLSI process technology and manufacturing equipment. The VLSI project had a four-year budget of approximately $250 million, of which 60% was paid for by the five principal research collaborators (Fujitsu, Hitachi, Mitsubishi, NEC, and Toshiba). The VLSI project was precompetitive in orientation; the goal was to enhance process capability rather than to develop specific product technologies. Approximately one third of the budget was used to purchase semiconductor manufacturing equipment from U.S. firms (Stowsky 1989). The VLSI consortium sought to learn how to produce and improve upon this equipment. By most accounts, the project was a tremendous success. Okimoto, Sugano, and Weinstein (1984) report that Japanese firms filed more than 1,000 patents, and published 460 research papers, on the basis of the collaborative research. Japanese electronics firms began in the early 1980s to establish an in-house capability in the manufacture of leading-edge process technology and equipment.

Even with advanced manufacturing capability, however, Japanese firms faced serious competitive problems, not the least of which was the need to capture a share of the U.S. market for semiconductor devices. In the mid-1970s, sales, to U.S. firms constituted approximately 60% of the total worldwide market for integrated circuits. In order to penetrate the U.S. market, however, Japanese producers had to deal with a serious image problem. Japan was widely perceived by U.S. electronics firms as a supplier of low-end products (so-called "jelly bean" devices), with little competence in technology-intensive products. The challenge facing Japanese semiconductor producers was not simply achieving parity in manufacturing but also convincing major U.S. firms that they could in fact match the performance of U.S. semiconductor suppliers.

U.S. semiconductor firms first felt the force of Japanese competition in the late 1970s. The window of opportunity was created by the failure of U.S. firms to match adequately production capacity to market demand. Following an industry-wide slump in semiconductor sales in 1974–75, U.S. firms reduced dramatically their capital investment in new production facilities. Capital expenditures by U.S. merchant semiconductor firms fell from $410 million in 1974, to just $194 million in 1975. When demand for semiconductors began to increase in 1977–78, shortages of production capacity rapidly emerged. Facing lengthy delivery delays, many high-volume U.S customers, such as Hewlett Packard and Xerox, turned to Japanese firms as an additional source of supply. Japanese firms began production of DRAMS in the late 1970s, using 16K DRAM circuit-designs licensed from U.S. semiconductor firms and manufacturing equipment purchased from U.S. equipment suppliers.[5] Following standard industry practice, U.S. semiconductor firms licensed Japanese producers as second-source suppliers. By the end of the 1970s, Japanese firms had captured 40% of the U.S. market for 16K DRAM devices.

This initial entry into the U.S. market was crucial to the subsequent success of Japanese firms. Sales to the United States allowed Japanese firms to engage in high-volume production of DRAM devices, creating the opportunity for realizing the kinds of economies of scale in production, learning economies, and improvements in manufacturing performance obtained by U.S. firms. Knowledge and information gained in the manufacture of 16K DRAMs was applied in the development of

---

[5]16K DRAMs were first sold on the open market by the U.S. firm Intel in late 1977.

subsequent generations of DRAM devices, initiating a process of cumulative learning. In addition, Japanese firms were able to demonstrate to U.S. customers the capability to match the production quality of international competitors. Indeed, for a brief period in the late 1970s, the production yields achieved by Japanese firms were actually higher than those of their U.S. competitors. Table 3.1 shows comparative data on failure rates for 16K DRAM devices manufactured by Japanese and U.S. firms. Using the same circuit design (licensed from Mostek), Japanese firms achieved much lower failure rates than U.S. producers. Testimony by Hewlett Packard engineers in 1980 gave wide publicity to the superior reliability of Japanese devices. While the quality differential in 16K DRAMs eventually narrowed, the success of Japan in this product market represented a dramatic challenge to the dominance of the United States in advanced integrated-circuit production.

Many U.S. merchant semiconductor producers apparently felt that the principal lesson to be learnt from the events of the late 1970s was the need to avoid a shortage of fabrication capacity; given the choice, they suggested, customers in the United States would still tend to purchase devices from U.S. rather than Japanese semiconductor suppliers. Far from abandoning or changing the manufacturing strategies that had proved successful in the 1970s, U.S. firms moved to construct additional dedicated high-volume production facilities. The top ten U.S. merchant semiconductor-producers invested in more than $2 billion worth of new production capacity in 1979–80 (Borrus, Millstein, and Zysman 1982). U.S. semiconductor firms fully expected to recapture in 64K and 256K DRAMs the market share they had lost in 16K devices.

TABLE 3.1. 16K DRAM Failure Rates (Parts per Million) for Japanese and U.S. Producers, 1978–82

	1978	1979	1980	1981	1982
Japanese producers	0.24	0.20	0.16	0.17	0.05
U.S. producers	1.00	1.32	0.78	0.18	0.02

Source: U.S. Congress, Office of Technology Assessment (1990).

Technology and Market Leadership

64K DRAMs were first offered for open-market sale in the United States in late 1980; 256K DRAMs were first available in commercial volume in 1983. Japanese and U.S. firms began manufacturing 1M DRAMs in 1986. In a dramatic reversal of the longstanding dominance of the United States in DRAM product and process technologies, Japanese firms were the first to enter volume merchant production of all three product designs.[6] Moreover, these new products were all based on Japanese product/process designs, as opposed to earlier generations of devices that were manufactured under second-source agreements with U.S. firms. Japanese firms had emerged as technology and production leaders in DRAM manufacturing.

Demand for DRAM circuits increased rapidly during the early 1980s, and both U.S., and Japanese firms were operating at close to full capacity. The market situation changed dramatically in 1985 as the electronics industry throughout the world, entered a deep recession that was to last until the middle of 1987. In an attempt to maintain sales volume, both U.S. and Japanese producers cut prices on semiconductor devices. The average price of 64K DRAM circuits fell from $4.00 in 1984, to approximately $1.00 in 1985. In the face of huge operating losses, Advanced Micro Devices, Intel, Mostek, Motorola, and National Semiconductor all withdrew from the DRAM market in 1985, leaving Texas Instruments and Micron Technology as the *only* U.S. merchant producers of DRAM devices.[7] The U.S. merchant semiconductor industry had, in effect, been driven out of this product market. By the end of the decade, Japanese firms held in excess of 70% of the world market for DRAM integrated circuits.

How did Japan achieve technology and market leadership?

---

[6]IBM was actually the first volume producer of all three products, but for in-house (captive) use only. The first volume merchant producers of 64K, 256K, and 1M DRAMs were Fujitsu, Hitachi, and Toshiba, respectively.

[7]Motorola subsequently reentered DRAM production in a joint-venture agreement with Toshiba of Japan. IBM manufactures DRAM devices, but for internal (captive) use only.

In contrast to the period of technology catch-up during the mid-1970s, the MITI led cooperative research effort was of only secondary importance.[8] Of far greater importance were differences in the structure of manufacturing systems in the United States and Japan. Perhaps the main difference was a commitment among Japanese semiconductor firms to production as a key area of manufacturing advantage, as opposed to the tendency in the United States to accord higher priority to product technology. Throughout the 1980s, Japanese semiconductor producers made substantial investments in automated production and assembly equipment, chemical purification, clean-room technology, process control, and the development of work practices that eliminated sources of device failure. One recent study by the U.S. Department of Commerce (1988), for example, estimated that in the mid-1980s Japanese semiconductor plants had a five-year lead over U.S. firms in the use of computer-integrated manufacturing techniques. According to this study, the use of computer automation allowed Japanese semiconductor firms to reduce production turnaround time by 42%, increase output by 50%, and increase equipment up-time by 25%.

More generally, however, competitive success derived from the tendency of Japanese firms to break with the bifurcated manufacturing forms typical of high-volume semiconductor production in the United States. The Japanese commitment to device performance and technological sophistication was balanced by a concern for the manufacturability of products and the development of product and process technologies that allowed for high yields in production. Typically, this involved the use of conservative circuit designs, scaling up from existing technology wherever possible. It also involved circuit designs with built-in redundancy to minimize device failure. Partly as a result of these strategies, Japanese firms were the first to achieve volume merchant production of 64K, 256K, and 1M DRAM devices, thereby capturing important

[8]Competition among Japanese firms dramatically intensified during the 1980s. Hitachi and Toshiba struggled for technology leadership in DRAM devices.

first-mover advantages in these product markets.[9] Most U.S. producers, by contrast, employed more complex circuit designs (e.g., pressing to a greater level of circuit density). Many of the new generations of DRAM devices introduced by U.S. firms encountered serious yield problems under factory conditions.[10]

Table 3.2 provides illustrative data on the yields achieved in 1M DRAM production by Toshiba and by a U.S. merchant firm in 1986 (the U.S. firm subsequently withdrew from the DRAM market). The costs of production (wafer cost, assembly and test cost, and so forth) of the two firms were broadly similar. Yields from wafer fabrication, however, were substantially higher at Toshiba (68%) than at the U.S. competitor (25%). The impact of the yield differential on final unit production cost was dramatic: $11.83 at the U.S. firm, $3.31 at Toshiba. The higher yield achieved by Toshiba reflected a series of intersecting factors. As an early entrant to volume production, Toshiba was further down the learning curve and had already fine-tuned the fabrication line to eliminate many sources of device failure. In addition, Toshiba used a relatively conservative circuit design (actually a scaled-up version of the previous generation of DRAM circuits). More generally, the high yields reflected the attention paid to quality control and

[9]First-mover advantages derive largely from the learning curve effect in semiconductor production: manufacturing yields tend to improve over time as firms resolve problems and difficulties on the production line. Production costs often fall by as much as 30% with each doubling of cumulative production volume. Firms that are the first to enter production are further down the learning curve and achieve higher yields and lower production costs relative to later entrants. In addition, late entrants often have difficulty convincing major end-users to switch from existing suppliers because the end-users have already incurred large certification costs in ensuring the quality of products from those suppliers.

[10]A report of the U.S. Congress's Office of Technology Assessment (1990, p. 96) describes the difficulties of one U.S. firm as follows: "Technical management and quality philosophy proved to be key problems for the U.S. firm. Its design engineers developed their DRAM process and prototypes in the laboratory, and then 'threw the design over the fence' to the manufacturing engineers. The design engineers recognized the difficulties of producing 1M DRAMs with their design: they attempted to compensate by specifying a high-quality starting wafer, by keeping the chip size relatively large, and by including a very large number of redundant memory cells on the chip as back-up. They were relying on inspection and correction after production to provide useable DRAMs, rather than designing quality in."

TABLE 3.2. 1M DRAM Manufacturing Cost Comparison for a U.S. and a Japanese Producer, 1986[a]

Operation	U.S. firm	Toshiba
Wafer cost[b]	$60.00	$25.00
Processed wafer cost	$335.00	$300.00
Chip size (square mm)	73	54
Total possible chips per 125mm wafer	151	205
Wafer probe yield (%)	25	68
Number of good chips	38	139
Packaging cost	$0.25	$0.25
Assembly yield (%)	92	92
Final test cost	$0.20	$0.20
Final test yield (%)	85	85
Total production cost	$11.83	$3.31

[a]Representative values for Toshiba of Japan and a merchant U.S. semiconductor firm that subsequently ceased DRAM operations.
[b]The U.S. firm used a higher-quality initial wafer (epitaxial).
Source: U.S. Congress, Office of Technology Assessment (1990).

the investment in production automation by Japanese semiconductor firms.

Close relations between semiconductor firms and equipment suppliers are another characteristic of semiconductor manufacturing in Japan that contributed to the success of Japanese firms in DRAM markets. During the 1960s and 1970s, the U.S. semiconductor industry had the advantage of early access to leading-edge equipment from domestic suppliers. Throughout the 1970s, U.S. firms dominated the market for semiconductor manufacturing equipment. Notwithstanding the significance of this linkage, however, relations between U.S. semiconductor firms and equipment suppliers were often strained. Rather than developing long-term partnership agreements with equipment suppliers, U.S. semiconductor firms switched among many competing firms in a search for the most advanced technology. In addition, U.S. semiconductor firms typically transferred much of the cost of fluctuating demand to their equipment suppliers in the form of canceled or reduced orders for capital equipment.

Stowsky (1989, p. 248) describes the status of the U.S. semiconductor equipment industry as follows:

most semiconductor equipment manufacturers remained small, undercapitalized and highly vulnerable to the economic and technological fortunes of the device sector. Their characteristic lack of communication with their major customers showed when the device makers' fortunes soured, for the first time, in the mid-seventies. Quick to double order in boom times, the device makers moved even faster to cancel during the bust. Still smarting from the shock, equipment makers were slow to respond to new orders from chipmakers during the 1977–78 recovery, and the enormous backlogs and stretched out delivery schedules that resulted just exacerbated the antagonism and mistrust that already existed between them.

Japanese producers, by contrast, formed strong partnerships with equipment suppliers, thereby facilitating investments in new equipment technologies and supporting the emergence of a strong equipment industry. Stowsky (1989, p. 253) describes these advantages in the following terms:

> device makers most often took the lead in promoting or introducing new equipment into the manufacturing process. . . . Manufacturing engineers and scientists employed by the device makers worked closely and routinely with their equipment suppliers to adapt equipment to the actual production environment in which it was expected to operate, prior to marketing the product. . . . Financial and ownership ties among semiconductor device and equipment firms provided a larger pool of investment capital than that available to independent equipment producers in the United States. . . .

As the costs of new equipment technology increased, it became increasingly difficult for small U.S. equipment manufacturers to compete, resulting in increasing Japanese dominance in equipment manufacturing. Between 1983 and 1989, the U.S. share of the worldwide market for wafer fabrication equipment declined from 62% to 41%; during the same time period, Japanese firms increased their market share from 28% to 48% (*Tokyo Business Today,* February 1990). In 1979, nine of the top ten semiconductor equipment manufacturers in the world (ranked by sales) were U.S. firms; in 1989, only four U.S. firms ranked in the top ten. Japanese firms have also been especially strong in the key area of lithography; the U.S. share of sales of semiconductor lithographic equipment fell from 71% in 1983, to 29% in 1988 (U.S. General Accounting Office [GAO] 1990). The lithography market is now dominated by two Japanese firms (Canon and Nikon). As Japan has emerged as the leading supplier of semiconductor manufacturing equipment, preexisting synergies between U.S. semiconductor firms and equipment suppliers have been eroded; it is now Japanese semiconductor firms that gain early access to leading-edge equipment.

Two sets of additional events helped to secure greater market share for Japanese firms. First, the large integrated-organization structure of Japanese semiconductor firms placed them in a stronger position, relative to U.S. merchant producers, for dealing with the recessionary conditions of the mid-1980s. During this period of declining sales and rapid price reductions, *both* U.S. and Japanese firms were selling at below manufacturing cost (U.S. International Trade Commission [USITC] 1986). It is estimated that during the 1985–86 recession, Japanese semiconductor firms suffered operating losses of approximately $4 billion. Japanese semiconductor firms, backed by capital investors, were apparently able and willing to incur these short-term losses in order to achieve the long-term goal of increasing market share within the United States.[11]

Figure 3.2 shows capital expenditures by U.S. merchant semiconductor firms and Japanese semiconductor firms during the period 1973–90. These data indicate that from 1983 onward, investments in new equipment and facilities by Japanese firms exceeded those of U.S. merchant producers. Notwithstanding large losses, Japanese firms continued a massive program of investment in new manufacturing facilities and equipment through the 1980s. During the period 1983–85, Japanese capital investments as a percentage of semiconductor sales were approximately twice those of U.S. merchant firms (Flamm

---

[11]As Dick (1991) suggests, what the International Trade Commission interpreted as dumping was actually consistent with the long-term goals of maximizing market share and profits over the complete life cycle of the product. If a large market share is captured, losses incurred early in the life cycle can be recouped through subsequent high-volume production.

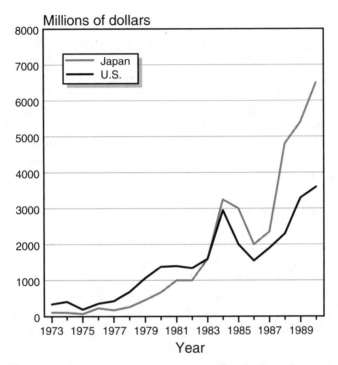

FIGURE 3.2. Capital expenditures by U.S. merchant semiconductor firms and Japanese semiconductor firms, 1973–90. (*Sources*: For the years 1973–80 adapted from Okimoto, D., Sugano, T., Weinstein, F. 1984. *Competitive Edge: The Semiconductor Industry in the United States and Japan.* Stanford, CT: Stanford University Press; for the years 1981–90 adapted from Integrated Circuit Engineering Corporation. 1992. *Status 1992.* Scottsdale, AZ: ICE.)

1991). Through this large-scale investment, Japanese firms built up capacity for leading-edge semiconductor manufacturing.

Second, Japanese firms have been able to sell semiconductor devices within a relatively protected domestic market, and at higher prices than in the United States. Throughout the 1960s and 1970s, U.S. firms were prevented from establishing wholly owned subsidiaries in Japan. Japanese electronics firms, sometimes with the encouragement of MITI (e.g., through the denial of import licenses), have tended to favor domestic semiconductor suppliers over international competitors, and this has limited the ability of the latter to gain substantial market share. According to the estimates of the U.S. industry, U.S. firms currently supply approximately 14% of the Japanese market. By way of comparison, Japanese firms hold 22% of the U.S. market.[12] Japan has experienced a trade surplus with the United States since 1980. In 1991, the trade surplus was $630 million, down from a peak of $1.5 billion in 1989 (the recent reduction is due in large part to the falling prices of DRAM devices).

The low levels of sales of U.S. firms in Japan have become especially significant as the Japanese market for DRAMs and other advanced integrated-circuit devices has experienced rapid growth. In 1982 Japan accounted for 28% of worldwide merchant semiconductor consumption; by 1991 Japanese semiconductor consumption totalled $24 billion, 38% of the worldwide market (ICE 1992). Japanese firms are now the largest consumers of integrated circuits in the world. While the Japanese semiconductor market continues to be dominated by consumer electronics (38%, by value, of end-use), much of the recent growth in demand has come from the computer industry, providing an additional market-pull influence on technology development for Japanese semiconductor firms.

While dominating their domestic market, Japanese firms have expanded their capability to manufacture advanced semiconductors in the United States. Figure 3.3 shows the location of Japanese-owned semiconductor fabrication facilities in the United States, During the mid-1980s, all of the major Japanese semiconductor firms opened fabrication facilities in the United States, primarily for the production of DRAM devices. There are currently sixteen Japanese-owned fabrication plants in the United States, along with numerous research and support facilities. The geography of Japanese-owned fabrication facilities is broadly similar to that of U.S. high-volume production

---

[12]There is considerable dispute between the United States and Japan on how market share should be calculated. The U.S. figure of 14% is based on data provided by U.S. suppliers and excludes captive production. Under the formula preferred by Japan, the U.S. share of the Japanese market is estimated to have been 16% in 1991; this market share includes semiconductors *sold* under a U.S. brand name but *produced* by a Japanese firm.

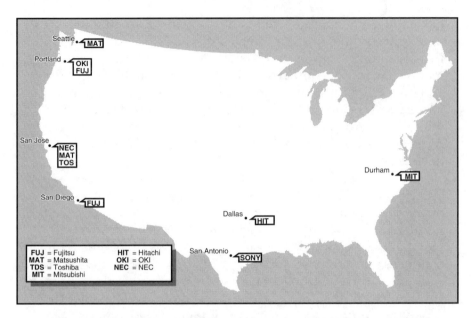

FIGURE 3.3. Location of Japanese-owned semiconductor production facilities in the United States, 1991.

plants; Japanese facilities are scattered across the western and southern United States. The presence of local production facilities has further enhanced the ability of Japanese firms to capture market share, providing just-in-time delivery and local service support to the U.S. computer industry and other major users of DRAM circuits.

THE INITIAL U.S. RESPONSE

The emergence of Japan as a major technological force profoundly changed the competitive conditions in the global semiconductor industry. Many aspects of established manufacturing practice that had previously contributed to the innovative dynamism of the U.S. semiconductor industry, such as the openness of the technology environment, became a source of competitive weakness under conditions of intensified global competition in the 1980s and thereafter. Leakage of technology from U.S. start-up firms to Japanese competitors emerged as a major problem. Norms of manufacturing performance sustained by U.S. semiconductor firms during the 1970s were no longer sufficient to secure market advantage. In retrospect, it is clear that leadership in the new era of global competition required fundamental changes in the way U.S. firms developed and produced semiconductor devices, including dramatic improvements in production yields and time-to-market for new technologies.

Requisite changes were slow in coming. For much of the 1980s, the restructuring of the U.S. semiconductor industry was dominated less by changes in manufacturing practice than by the redeployment of manufacturing resources away from DRAMs and other commodity devices (where Japan is especially dominant) and into more design-intensive product markets, such as microprocessors, mixed-signal devices, and very fast logic devices. Most of the major U.S. merchant semiconductor firms have now refocused their manufacturing strategies on these so-called value-added devices. In large part, these strategies involve a search for markets in which the innovative capability of U.S. firms in product design offsets Japanese leadership in high-volume manufacturing and process technology. Commodity products are increasingly used by large firms primarily as process drivers; the bulk of manufacturing capacity is devoted to design-intensive markets where profit margins are typically higher.[13]

U.S. semiconductor manufacturers also sought a political solution to the competitive challenge by claiming that Japanese firms should be penalized for unfair trading practices. In response to requests from U.S. semiconductor firms, the U.S. International Trade Commission in 1984 initiated an investigation of the reported "dumping" of 64K DRAMs in the U.S. market. Under the terms of the 1930 Tariff Act, the Commission sought to determine whether Japanese semiconductor manufacturers were selling DRAM chips in the United States at

---

[13]The emphasis placed on design-intensive products paid major dividends in the late 1980s. U.S. firms were to a significant degree sheltered from the intensive price competition in DRAMs brought on by the entry of South Korean firms into that market.

less than fair value (LTFV), with fair value being defined as the price required to gain a normal rate of return from the production and sale of DRAM devices. In June 1986 the Commission reported that Japanese manufacturers were selling DRAMs at a weighted average of 20.75% LTFV, and it instructed the Customs Service to impose punitive tariffs on imports from these firms (USITC 1986). The decision itself was the subject of considerable controversy, with several commissioners arguing that the rapid price declines of DRAMs were a normal feature of semiconductor pricing over the product cycle rather than the result of dumping by Japanese firms. In addition, since the Commission found both Japanese *and* U.S. firms selling DRAMs at below actual production cost, the LTFV calculations were based on a set of estimated rather than actual prices, further fueling the dispute concerning the normal pricing schedule for semiconductor devices.

As it happened, the imposition of tariffs was averted when an accord was signed by U.S. and Japanese trade representatives in 1986. The accord had two main elements. First, it put in place a process for establishing fair-value prices on DRAMs and other memory devices; Japanese manufacturers agreed to maintain prices above these levels. This element of the accord addressed the principal U.S. concern—dumping by Japanese manufacturers—and resulted in a stabilization, and even a slight increase, in unit prices for DRAM devices throughout the second half of the 1980s. Second, the accord set a target for increased semiconductor sales by U.S. firms in Japan (20% of the Japanese market). The exact significance of the 20% target immediately emerged as a focus of dispute. U.S. negotiators interpreted the accord as a guarantee that Japan would increase its consumption of U.S. semiconductors to the 20% level. Japanese negotiators interpreted the figure as a goal that might or might not be met, depending on the demand for U.S. semiconductor products in Japan.

In any event, the 1986 U.S.–Japan semiconductor trade agreement had little direct impact on the competitiveness of U.S. semiconductor firms. With respect to the issue of dumping, the best that can be argued is that by placing constraints on price competition, the trade agreement created a breathing space within which U.S. firms could address their underlying problems of production quality, yields, and turnaround time on new products. While Japanese firms held back from aggressive pricing of DRAMs, this restraint had only a minimal influence on the market share held by U.S. merchant firms since all U.S. merchant manufacturers, with the exception of Texas Instruments and Micron Technology, had already withdrawn from the product market. Japanese manufacturers who remained in the market benefitted from stable prices until the late 1980s, when South Korean firms began a new round of price cuts.[14] On the issue of opening up Japanese markets, an area in which the U.S. government arguably could make a significant contribution to the profitability of U.S. semiconductor firms, the 1986 agreement was a manifest failure. Although the share of the Japanese market held by U.S. firms increased marginally during the second half of the 1980s, the basic trade problem remained.

While U.S. firms continued to lose market share in DRAMs, assessments of the competitive prospects of U.S. firms were clouded by changes in manufacturing technologies, and most especially by the development of application-specific semiconductor devices. Application-specific integrated circuits (primarily gate arrays and standard cells) offer a relatively inexpensive method for producing small batches of integrated circuits designed to meet the explicit needs of a customer. Because these devices are designed for individual users, their value derives in large part from the quality of the design and efficiencies in low-volume manufacturing rather than from the mass-production strategies that are characteristic of DRAM manufacture. In contrast to the large dedicated facilities used in DRAM production, manufacturers of application-specific

---

[14]The U.S.–Japanese semiconductor agreement appears to have had an effect on pricing that extended beyond DRAMs to other commodity products. The stabilization of prices emerged as a source of contention between producers and users of semiconductors in the United States. Computer manufacturers and other high-volume users argued that higher component prices would hurt their competitiveness in global markets. When a second round of semiconductor trade negotiations was initiated in 1991, attention shifted away from dumping and price stabilization and toward the problem of market access, allowing U.S. high-technology firms to present a united front in their lobbying efforts with U.S trade negotiators.

circuits have developed smaller modular facilities that are oriented to low-volume production (Angel 1990).

Once again, it was U.S. start-up companies that pioneered the development and deployment of applications specific devices. Like the merchant producers of earlier generations, virtually all of these start-up integrated-circuit firms were established in Silicon Valley (Rice 1987b). Table 3.3 identifies U.S. semiconductor firms that began operation in Silicon Valley during the period 1977–86. Approximately one third of these start-up firms were founded to manufacture application-specific semiconductors; others focused on emerging markets for custom-memory and gallium arsenide devices (Angel 1990). Of the new start-ups, VLSI Technology, LSI Logic, Linear Technology, IMP, Cypress, and Sierra Semiconductor have become a major new force in the manufacture of application-specific circuits. More recent start-ups, such as Vitelic and

TABLE 3.3. Semiconductor Firms Founded in Santa Clara County, 1977–86

Year	Semiconductor firms
1977	California Micro Devices
1978	Acrian, California Devices, Custom MOS, Micrel, Oki, Universal Semiconductor, Xicor
1979	American Valence, Metelics, VLSI Technology
1980	Dielectric Semiconductor, Integrated Device Technology, Harris Microwave, LSI Logic
1981	IMP, Linear Technology, Seeq, Telmos, Weitek
1982	Array Technology, Calogic, Custom MOS Arrays, SenSym
1983	Altera, American Micro-Components, Cypress, Elantec, Exel, International CMOS Technology, IXYS, Laserpath, Micro-Linear, Modular Semiconductor, Sierra Semiconductor, Visic, Vitelic, Wafer Scale Integration, Zytrex
1984	Alliance Semiconductor, Atmel, Chips and Technologies, Cirrus Logic, Compound Semiconductors, Inova Microelectronics, Integrated CMOS Systems, KMOS Semi-Custom, Pacific Monoliths, Saratoga Semiconductor, Vitesse
1985	Advanced Linear Devices, Catalyst Semiconductor, Celeritek, Maxim Integrated Products, Topaz, Tri-Star Semiconductor
1986	Austek Microsystems, Micro Integration, Panatech, S-MOS Systems, Zoran

Atmel, are leading the drive into new product markets in custom and semicustom integrated circuits. The success of application-specific device manufacturers, as well as of Intel and other value-added producers, fueled new rounds of growth in Silicon Valley. Semiconductor employment in Silicon Valley reached an all-time high of 52,300 in September 1984.[15]

The withdrawal of U.S. semiconductor firms from intensely competitive commodity-price markets, and the increasing emphasis on so-called value-added manufacturing, involved a major redeployment of the manufacturing capacity of U.S. semiconductor firms. It did not, however, involve a fundamental reorientation of the manufacturing form. U.S. manufacturers continued to emphasize technology development. Much of the bifurcation of innovation and production remained. Indeed, in the case of many merchant firms, the organizational and geographical separation of development and production increased. Most new start-up firms in the application-specific product market subcontracted out their wafer fabrication requirements to so-called silicon foundries that service the demands of a number of different semiconductor producers. The rapidly rising costs of new submicron production facilities forced start-up firms to depend on outside suppliers. For example, Weitek, a start-up manufacturer of application-specific circuits, subcontracts out its wafer fabrication to two Silicon Valley semiconductor firms (VLSI Technology and Intel), and to Toshiba Semiconductor in Japan.

In the context of intensified international competition, additional weaknesses were exposed in this entrepreneurial mode of industrialization. Lacking adequate financing, and with only uncertain access to advanced fabrication-capacity, many start-up firms entered into partnership agreements with foreign competitors. During the 1980s, the majority of U.S. start-up firms formed production alliances with Japanese firms. Table 3.4 shows a sample of the agreements established between U.S. start-up producers and Japanese firms during the

[15]Industry recessions in 1985–86 and 1989–90, and rationalization of manufacturing capacity in response to Japanese competition, subsequently led to a major reduction in employment. Total semiconductor employment in Silicon Valley was just over 41,000 at the end of 1990.

TABLE 3.4. Sample Alliances between U.S. Semiconductor Start-ups and Japanese Firms

Japanese firms	U.S. partner	Reiationship
Fujitsu	Vitesse	Joint development (GaAs)
Hitachi	VLSI Technology	Production (SRAMs)
Kawasaki Steel	LSI Logic	Joint venture (SRAMs)
NKK	Paradigm	Production (SRAMs)
Nippon Steel	VLSI Technology	Joint venture (ASICs)
Oki Electric	Vitelic	Production (ASICs)
Ricoh	Plus Logic	Production (ASICs)

1980s. Most of the alliances were formed between U.S. start-up firms and large Japanese electronics manufacturers. An interesting additional feature of this alliance formation, however, is the establishment of joint ventures between U.S. start-ups and such Japanese steel companies as Kawasaki Steel, NKK, and Nippon Steel. For these latter firms, alliances with U.S. start-ups are a low-cost strategy for diversifying into high-technology production.

In all, more than 1,000 alliances were established between U.S. semiconductor producers and Japanese firms during the 1980s. These alliances have taken many forms, from licensing and marketing of technology, to joint production of semiconductor devices. While the prevalence of different types of alliances varies from year to year, data for 1990 indicate that the most common alliances involve technology development agreements, marketing agreements, and fabrication agreements. The latter category of agreements characterizes alliances in which one semiconductor firm agrees to serve as the production foundry for another. Fabrication agreements proliferated in the 1980s because of the emergence of large numbers of vertically disintegrated U.S. firms that lacked in-house fabrication capacity.

While several well-publicized alliances were formed with large U.S. merchant producers (e.g., that between Motorola and Toshiba for DRAM production), the majority of alliances have been between large Japanese firms and small U.S. start-up companies, including semiconductor producers, equipment manufacturers, and design tool houses. Of particular concern are agreements that involve an exchange of leading-edge product technology for guaranteed access to production capability. As a recent report from the National Research Council (1992) has indicated, these agreements have accelerated the flow of technological knowledge to Japan, thereby allowing Japanese firms to gain access to new market segments, such as those of gate arrays, SRAMs, and mixed-signal devices.

CONCLUSION

Global competition now extends across all aspects of the semiconductor industry, from design tools to integrated circuits and production equipment. Table 3.5 presents a summary of the relative competitive position of Japan and the United States in key areas of technology development and manufacturing practice in the late 1980s. While U.S. firms have retained a leadership position in some important products (especially microprocessors), in automated design technologies, and in software development, the overall trend has been toward an erosion of U.S. technological advantage by Japanese firms. Japan has emerged as the largest supplier of semiconductors in the world, the largest market for semiconductor devices, and the dominant supplier of several key enabling technologies. As this has occurred, Japanese semiconductor firms have been able to realize the kinds of synergies among local producers, customers, and suppliers that were once only available to U.S. firms.[16]

During the mid-1980s, Japanese semiconductor firms diversified from DRAM production into a variety of other product markets, including low-density application-specific circuits. As this occurred, it became increasingly clear that competitive success required a more fundamental restructuring of the U.S. semiconductor industry. Two primary problems had to be addressed. The first concerned enduring problems of yield and

[16]Several U.S. firms (e.g., Texas Instruments) are now locating semiconductor R&D facilities in Japan in attempt to tap into localized knowledge systems in that country.

TABLE 3.5. Competitive Position of Japan and the United States in Semiconductor Technologies, Late 1980s

	U.S. lead	Equal	Japanese lead
Devices			
Memory ICs			*
Microprocessors	*		
ASICs		*	
Optoelectronics			*
Semiconductor packaging			*
Automatic test equipment			*
Automatic assembly		*	
Enabling technology			
Chemical deposition		*	
Ion implantation	*		
Optical lithography		*	
Plasma etch			*
Computer-aided design	*		
Clean room			*
Computer integrated production			*
Materials			
Silicon			*
Gallium arsenide			*
Ultrapure chemicals			*

Source: U.S. Congress, Office of Technology Assessment (1990).

quality in the production process. U.S. firms simply could not compete using manufacturing practices that generated production yields less than half those of Japanese semiconductor firms. The second involved translating the innovative capability of U.S. firms into market share by shortening the time-to-market on new products and production processes. How these problems have been addressed is the subject of subsequent chapters of this book.

CHAPTER 4

Restructuring for Global Competition

If one event were to signify the end of an era in the history of the U.S. semiconductor industry, it would be the sale of Fairchild Semiconductor in early 1987. One of the founding semiconductor firms in Silicon Valley, and the parent of a multitude of successful spin-off producers, Fairchild had symbolized the technologically dynamic forms of industrialization that emerged in the U.S. semiconductor industry beginning in the late 1950s. Like those of many other medium-size merchant semiconductor firms, the fortunes of the company went into a downward spiral in the 1980s, marked by a loss of market share and declining profits on major product lines. In late 1986, the Japanese firm Fujitsu sought to acquire Fairchild Semiconductor from the French parent firm Schlumberger. The proposed take-over generated widespread opposition in the United States; notwithstanding its competitive difficulties in commercial markets, Fairchild remained a major supplier of technology to the U.S. military. Under pressure from the U.S. government, Fujitsu withdrew its offer.[1] Fairchild Semiconductor was eventually sold to National Semiconductor.

[1]The proposed sale of Fairchild Semiconductor to Fujitsu was only the latest example of foreign acquisition of U.S. high-technology firms. In the face of widespread fears of technology dependency, Congress passed the Exon–Florio amendment authorizing the president to block mergers with, or acquisitions of, U.S. firms by foreign companies when such transactions would threaten U.S. national security. Of the more than 750 foreign acquisitions reported to the President's Committee on Foreign Investments, however, only 14 have been investigated, and only 1 (a sale to China) was blocked on national security grounds.

Fairchild was not the only U.S. semiconductor firm to experience competitive difficulties. While many specialized start-up firms grew rapidly during the second half of the 1980s, intense price competition in commodity markets undermined the profitability of most large and medium-size U.S. merchant semiconductor firms.[2] For example, Advanced Micro Devices reported a loss of $64 million in 1987, and of $54 million in 1990. Employment at the company fell from just over 18,000 in 1987, to 12,000 in 1990. National Semiconductor lost money every year during the period 1989–91; total revenue on semiconductors in 1991 was less than that in 1985. These losses were incurred despite large increases in worldwide demand for advanced semiconductors. During the period 1983–90, the total worldwide employment of the U.S. semiconductor industry fell by more than 25,000.

The problems facing the U.S. semiconductor industry during the 1980s were large and complex. Low yields and fluctuating capacity utilization undermined the ability of U.S. firms to retain market share in intensely price-competitive commodity device markets. At the same time, competition from Japan challenged the longstanding advantage of U.S. firms in product and process technology. The competitive problems of U.S. firms were further compounded by the rising capital and R&D costs of manufacturing advanced integrated circuits; the price of a high-volume fabrication facility approximately tripled during the 1980s. Wafer-thin profits were insufficient to support the requisite reinvestment in new facilities and production lines, forcing rationalization of manufacturing capacity. The growing importance of foreign markets, and of foreign equipment suppliers, created additional difficulties for U.S. semiconductor firms. In the face of these competitive challenges, most observers predicted a bleak future for the U.S. semiconductor industry.

The competitive status of the industry remains precarious in the 1990s. And yet the anticipated collapse of the industry has not occurred. The manufacturing performance of U.S. firms has improved dramatically. Market share has stabilized. Cycle-time for the development of new products and production processes has been substantially reduced. Moreover, it is

---

[2]The major exception was Intel. Intel's major microprocessor product-lines were not subject to commodity pricing during the 1980s.

possible to make the case that U.S. firms are positioned for further recovery in the 1990s. By emphasizing the rapid development and deployment of advanced design-intensive devices, U.S. firms have avoided much of the intense price competition that has emerged in high-volume commodity markets and have managed to establish a leadership position in emerging product-lines, such as mixed-signal devices and RISC microprocessors.

This stabilization of economic fortunes reflects a fundamental restructuring of the U.S. semiconductor industry. In what follows, I examine the major dimensions of change in manufacturing practice and industrial structure, drawing on the results of a questionnaire survey and lengthy interviews with senior executives and engineering staff of U.S. semiconductor firms. Details of the survey, and the characteristics of the sample firms, are provided in the Appendix.

Two dominant themes emerge from the analysis. The first is the increasing "Japanization" of U.S. manufacturing systems—involving, in particular, much closer cooperative ties among customers, semiconductor producers, and equipment suppliers—and the creation of multidimensional product teams as the key agents of change in production. U.S. firms have learned from their Japanese competitors, just as the latter learned the techniques of semiconductor manufacturing from U.S. firms decades before; the result has been a convergence of the manufacturing performance of U.S. and Japanese firms. The second theme of the analysis is the increasing integration of technology development and production within U.S. semiconductor firms; the previously fragmented manufacturing form has been transformed in ways that allow a more rapid deployment of new technologies and the achievement of enhanced yields in production. In its clearest articulation, integration involves the physical combination of product development and production within individual manufacturing facilities. The resultant geography is markedly different from the previously dominant spatial and international divisions of labor within high-technology manufacturing systems.

THE STRUCTURE OF THE INDUSTRY

It is useful at this point to provide an overview of the current structure of the U.S. semiconductor industry. My analysis focuses on the manufacture of integrated circuits rather than of older discrete-device technology.

As of mid-1991, there were 145 U.S. firms actively manufacturing integrated circuits of various types. Worldwide sales of integrated circuits by these firms in 1990 totalled $23.2 billion; merchant producers accounted for $17.4 billion (75%) of these sales, and "captive" firms for $5.8 billion (25%) (Integrated Circuit Engineering Corporation [ICE] 1992). Merchant producers are defined as firms that manufacture semiconductors primarily for external, or open-market, sales; this group of firms includes both diversified electronics conglomerates, such as AT&T and Harris, as well as specialized semiconductor producers, such as Advanced Micro Devices and LSI Logic. Captive producers (e.g., IBM and Digital Equipment Corporation) manufacture semiconductors primarily for in-house use; typically, the electronics divisions of these firms also purchase semiconductors on the open market (the percentage of semiconductors produced in-house varies from a high of 85% to a low of 10%).

Table 4.1 ranks U.S. semiconductor firms by sales of integrated circuits in 1990. Three broad groups of firms may be identified. The first group comprises six firms (five merchant and one captive), each with integrated-circuit shipments in 1990 valued at more than $1 billion. The largest U.S. manufacturer of integrated circuits is the captive semiconductor (advanced technology) division of IBM. While IBM currently manufactures semiconductors exclusively for in-house use, the company has recently announced its intention to begin merchant sales of DRAM devices, microprocessors, and other advanced integrated circuits.[3] Advanced Micro Devices, Motorola, National Semiconductor, and Texas Instruments are all

---

[3]Merchant semiconductor sales are part of a fundamental organizational restructuring currently underway at IBM, DEC, Hewlett Packard, and other large, vertically integrated electronics firms. IBM's highly centralized and integrated organizational structure is being abandoned in favor of a series of semiautonomous product and technology divisions, each of which may sell on the open market. In addition to merchant sales of semiconductors, IBM has also begun external sales of manufacturing equipment (e.g., scanning microscopes), computer disc and tape drives, and other component technologies. Total worldwide employment at IBM has fallen by more than 100,000 since the mid-1980s.

TABLE 4.1. U.S. Integrated Circuit Manufacturers, Ranked by Sales Volume, 1990

	Merchant	Captive
Shipments of >$1 billion	Intel Motorola Texas Instruments National Semiconductor Advanced Micro Devices	IBM
Shipments >$200 million <$1 billion	AT&T Harris LSI Logic Analog Devices VLSI Technology Cypress Semiconductor Micron Technology Western Digital	DEC Hewlett Packard Delco (GM) Rockwell

Shipments <$200 million	Atmel
	Burr-Brown
	CMD, IDT, IMP
	Linear Tech, NCR
	Silicon Systems
	Siliconix, Xilinx,
	  and 100 other firms
		Commodore
		Cray Computer
		  and 14 other
		  firms

broadly based semiconductor firms with interests in a wide range of commodity and specialized markets. The semiconductor shipments of Intel, the last firm in this group, are dominated by its 80x86 series of microprocessors. Jointly, these six firms in 1990 were responsible for approximately 65% of total integrated-circuit shipments by U.S.-based firms.

The second group of producers in Table 4.1 had integrated-circuit sales in 1990 of between $200 million and $1 billion. Typically, these firms maintain advanced design and fabrication capability but are focused on a limited set of product markets and process technologies. Of particular note in this regard are the firms Cypress Semiconductor, LSI Logic, and VLSI Technology, which have been at the forefront in the development of new design-intensive integrated circuits, such as high-integration gate arrays and very fast SRAM (static random-access memory) devices. In general, these mid-size firms tend to avoid high-volume commodity markets in favor of value-added market niches. The principal exception is Micron Technology, which manufactures DRAMs and other advanced memory-devices. Among captive firms, Digital Equipment Corporation and Hewlett Packard manufacture substantial volumes of advanced integrated circuits for use in computer and communication systems.

In addition to these two groups of firms, there are many smaller producers that typically have narrow product foci and technology emphases (e.g., gallium arsenide devices, analog circuits, custom memory devices, and so forth). Many of these small producers are design houses; the actual fabrication and assembly of their semiconductor devices are performed by external subcontractors. Most of the captive firms in this group maintain in-house manufacturing capacity for semiconductors only for product development; volume production is carried out by external merchant producers. The large number of specialized small producers remains a distinguishing feature of the U.S. semiconductor industry; in Europe and Japan, semiconductor manufacturing is dominated by large electronics conglomerates.

In terms of sales volume, small semiconductor producers are only of secondary importance, collectively accounting for approximately 15%–20% of total merchant integrated-circuit production. This sales percentage, however, understates the significance of small firms to the vitality of the U.S. semiconductor industry. Small firms are usually start-up ventures set up to exploit new technologies. Many of these firms are on the leading edge of new product-technology development and are growing rapidly. Large producers often license technologies from these start-up firms to complement and extend their in-house technological capability. As discussed in Chapter 2, start-up firms have played a key role in extending important technological advances into new products and new market areas. While many of the technologies explored by start-up firms fail, the combined activity of multiple producers serves to broaden and deepen the technology pathways explored by U.S. semiconductor firms.

In addition to varying in size and product line, U.S. semiconductor firms can be distinguished by other dimensions of the manufacturing process. The most widely used classification differentiates between firms involved in the manufacture of standard products, on one hand, and of customer-specific devices, on the other. Whereas standard products are sold to many different users, customer-specific devices are designed and manufactured for one end-user only, thereby providing the latter firm with a proprietary component technology. Perhaps the most well known standard products are the 80 × 86 microprocessors manufactured by Intel and sold to multiple vendors of "clone" computers. The immediate significance of this standard product-custom product classification lies in the different supplier-customer relations associated with the products; custom devices typically involve much greater contact between the semiconductor supplier and the end-user. In addition, because standard products are often manufactured in high volume, competitive advantage in these product markets is often determined by economies of scale in production. Many standard products are so-called commodity devices; these are broadly similar component technologies that are available from multiple vendors who compete with one another to offer the best price and delivery schedule. It is, above all, in these commodity markets that Japanese expertise in high-volume automated production has been of greatest significance, and the competitive difficulties of U.S. merchant firms have been most severe.[4]

Until the mid-1970s, semiconductor manufacturing was dominated by standard products; custom designed circuits were limited to large end-users who had sufficient production volume to offset up-front design and development costs, and to

[4]Not all high-volume standard products have been subject to commodity pricing. For much of the 1980s, for example, Intel maintained a near technological-monopoly over microprocessor manufacturing for its de facto industry-standard 80 × 86 product line. In the absence of major competitors, Intel was able to maintain high prices and reap huge profits from the manufacture of microprocessors and allied products (e.g., floating point processors). During the late 1980s, Intel responded to the emergence of microprocessor clones (from Advanced Micro Devices, Chips and Technologies, and Cyrix) with price cuts, an accelerated rate of new product development, and aggressive enforcement of intellectual-property rights.

defense contractors. During the 1980s, however, the introduction of a series of new design and product technologies dramatically reduced the costs of producing advanced custom-integrated circuits in low volume, thus permitting more widespread use of custom products. Of greatest significance was the development of application-specific technologies, such as standard cells and gate arrays. Application-specific devices have provided computer manufacturers and other end-users with new opportunities to build proprietary component technology into electronic systems, and thereby to distinguish their products from those of competitors. In addition, Application-Specific Integrated Circuits (ASIC) technology has allowed computer firms and other electronics manufacturers to reduce development time on new system-technology, an issue of growing importance in high-technology industries. Many U.S. semiconductor firms now specialize in the manufacture of application-specific products, and application-specific devices currently represent approximately 18% of worldwide sales of integrated circuits. In contrast to the high-volume manufacturing strategies used for commodity products, application-specific circuits involve a greater emphasis on the use of sophisticated circuit-design tools and capability in low-volume flexible manufacturing. Wafer fabrication facilities are designed to run large numbers of process and product combinations on the same production line.

The rapid growth of application-specific product markets has stimulated significant advances in the technology, software, and manufacturing equipment required to design, produce, and test very high integration circuits in low-volume production. Using advanced design tools, single wafer processing systems, and automated modular-production facilities, U.S. semiconductor firms have been able to reduce dramatically the turnaround time and cost of designing and producing high-integration circuits. LSI Logic has reported a reduction in prototype development time from eight weeks in 1982, to two weeks in 1990; the length of the manufacturing cycle (from design to final test) has been cut in half. New advances in flexible manufacturing systems are likely to cut the costs of low-volume production and reduce turnaround time still further in the next decade (Steinmueller 1992; Langlois 1992).

The market for ASIC products per se has not grown as rapidly as many industry observers projected. Rather, as the capability for low-volume manufacturing has emerged, U.S. semiconductor firms have broadened the use of new technologies beyond customer-specific products and into the manufacture of standard products, or what are currently called application-specific standard products (ASSP). LSI Logic, for example, uses its proprietary design tools and gate-array process technology to manufacture hard-disk controller circuits that are sold to multiple end-users. ASIC technology is now viewed less as a set of customer-specific products than as an approach to manufacturing semiconductors of all types (from microprocessors to graphics chips) for individual customers and for open-market sales.

In the context of these developments in manufacturing technologies and market demand, the most relevant distinction in the semiconductor industry is not that between standard products and customer-specific products, but that between two manufacturing strategies, one focused on high-volume, routinized production, the other on design-intensive products and flexible manufacturing. These two manufacturing strategies are, however, less discrete alternatives than are the endpoints on a continuum ranging between different levels of production flexibility, market specificity, and dependence on product-specific economies of scale as the primary source of competitive advantage. Application-specific standard products and the use of "master slice" gate-array technologies represent intermediate positions on the continuum.[5] Currently, the primary commodity products are DRAMs, low- to medium-speed SRAMs, EPROMs (erasable programmable read-only memories), and standard logic circuits at small- and medium-scale integration. These products are typically produced in very high volume in large, capital-intensive fabrication facilities. Notwithstanding the growth in ASIC and ASSP production, there remains a huge demand for commodity products for use in computers, communications equipment, consumer electron-

---

[5]One approach to ASIC manufacturing involves customization of only the final layers of multilayer gate-array devices. Prior to customization, the basic device architecture is built up as a standard product (the master slice) and manufactured on a high-volume production line.

ics, and other high-volume markets. The product-specific econ-omies of scale associated with high-volume production contin-ue to drive down the price of commodity devices, making them the product of choice for cost-sensitive electronics systems for consumer and industrial markets[6].

The general tendency among U.S. firms has been to deem-phasize commodity products, on which competition from Japan and South Korea is strongest, in favor of high-integra-tion, design-intensive products produced with advanced design tools and flexible manufacturing technologies. Most large U.S. merchant semiconductor firms engage in both high-volume and flexible production for a wide variety of product markets. In recent years these firms have used high-volume commodity production as a vehicle for improving manufacturing efficiency and process technology, while devoting a high proportion of their manufacturing capacity to higher-margin, noncommodity products. At the same time, the majority of small and medium-size firms have emphasized flexible manufacturing and special-ized market and technology expertise, with actual volumes ranging from low- to medium-scale production.

The shift away from commodity products has provided some immediate relief from intense price competition and has helped to bolster the profitability of U.S. merchant semicon-ductor firms.[7] Design-intensive products do not, however, pro-vide a place to hide from global competition; the knowledge and technology necessary to compete in ASIC and ASSP mar-kets is now rapidly diffusing among semiconductor firms throughout the world. To remain competitive in the long run,

[6]By one industry estimate, approximately one third (by value) of integrated circuit sales are for high-volume products, such as VCRs, televisions, and personal computers (U.S. Congress, Committee on Government Affairs 1989). The National Advisory Com-mittee on Semiconductors contends that the long-term competitiveness of the U.S. semiconductor industry is dependent on the ability of the United States to establish a major market position in next-generation, high-volume electronics markets, such as high-definition television and multimedia communications equipment (NACS 1992).

[7]The movement away from commodity products has been the subject of intense debate within the industry. Quite apart from the sales volume associated with commodity markets, critics point to the role of commodity products as a vehicle for improving process technologies, yield enhancement, chemical purification, and other aspects of the manufacturing process.

U.S. firms must attain international standards of production performance and accelerate their rate of product and process technology development. The challenge is to establish manufacturing forms that permit high-quality production under conditions of continuous innovation and rapid technological change.

The Geography of Production

Figure 4.1 shows the location of semiconductor fabrication facilities in the United States in 1991. Notwithstanding the closure of older production facilities and the ongoing dispersal of fabrication capacity away from Silicon Valley, the region is still home to the largest concentration of semiconductor fabrication plants in the United States. Of the 144 fabrication facilities shown in Figure 4.1, 44 (30.6%) are located in Silicon Valley. Most large, high-volume production facilities (the so-called mega-fabs) are located outside of Silicon Valley (in Colorado, New Mexico, Texas, Utah, and elsewhere). In this re-

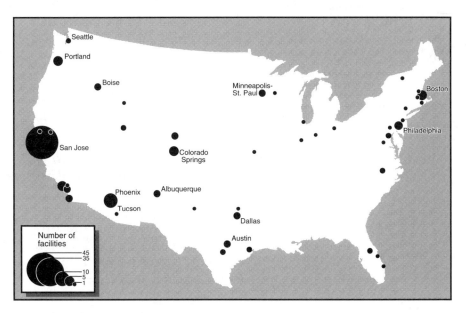

FIGURE 4.1. Location of semiconductor fabrication facilities in the United States, 1991.

gard, Silicon Valley's significance as a center of semiconductor production is somewhat overstated when measured in terms of the number of facilities as opposed to production capacity. When measured in terms of production capacity, Silicon Valley accounts for approximately 20% of semiconductor production in the United States. Silicon Valley remains, however, an important center for advanced development work and low-volume production. Advanced Micro Devices (AMD) is illustrative of large Silicon Valley-based merchant semiconductor firms in this regard. During the 1980s, AMD closed its older production lines in Silicon Valley and shifted its high-volume production to newer production facilities in Austin, Texas. AMD's most advanced manufacturing capability is still located in Silicon Valley, however, at its submicron development center in Sunnyvale (a $450 million manufacturing facility). Among the small and medium-size specialized producers, Integrated Device Technology, LSI Logic, Paradigm, and VLSI Technology all maintain advanced production capability in Silicon Valley.

The manufacturing operations of many U.S. semiconductor firms are international in scope. Figure 4.2 and Figure 4.3 show the location of fabrication facilities operated by U.S.-based firms in Europe and the Middle East, and in Japan, respectively. In general, only large and medium-size U.S. firms (IBM, Intel, LSI Logic, Motorola, Texas Instruments) maintain offshore wafer-fabrication facilities. The largest numbers of the facilities are in the United Kingdom and Germany. U.S. firms currently operate a total of six fabrication facilities in Japan (Texas Instruments has the greatest manufacturing presence in the region, including fabrication facilities in Ibaraki, Oita, and Saitama provinces, and a new R&D center in Tsukuba).

Note that Figures 4.2 and 4.3 provide data on manufacturing facilities owned by U.S. firms. In practice, much additional wafer fabrication is performed offshore, on a subcontract basis, by European, Japanese, and South Korean firms. The research firm Integrated Circuit Engineering Corporation estimates that approximately 60% of all subcontract semiconductor fabrication is performed in Japan and South Korea (ICE 1992).

While the production of semiconductor devices has a

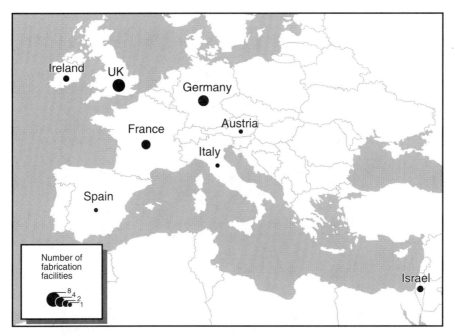

FIGURE 4.2. Semiconductor fabrication facilities operated by U.S. firms in Europe and the Middle East.

rather complex geography, Silicon Valley remains the locus for design and development work carried out by start-up firms in the U.S. semiconductor industry. Figure 4.4 shows the location of U.S.-based integrated circuit design houses (i.e., firms that subcontract out all production to external suppliers, or foundries). Note that Figure 4.4 does not include data on design consultants and on vendors of design tools who do not sell semiconductors under their own brand name. Of the forty-nine firms shown in Figure 4.4, thirty-seven (75.5%) are located in Silicon Valley. By clustering together in Silicon Valley, these start-up firms are able to realize significant external economies of scale in production (see Chapter 2).

RESTRUCTURING FOR GLOBAL COMPETITION

In what follows I examine in detail the changes that have occurred in the industrial structure and manufacturing prac-

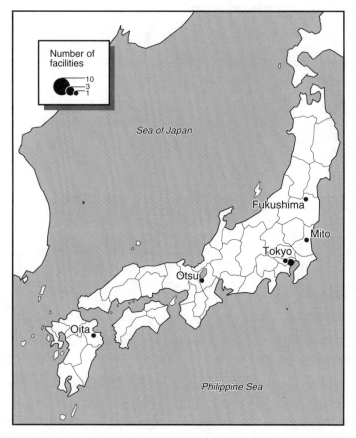

FIGURE 4.3. Semiconductor fabrication facilities operated by U.S. firms in Japan.

tices of U.S. firms since the mid-1980s. The analysis proceeds in two stages. In the remainder of this chapter, I describe the strategies used by U.S. semiconductor firms to improve manufacturing performance and reduce time-to-market on new technologies. In Chapter 5, I consider a second key dimension of organizational restructuring, namely, the formation of technology and production alliances between semiconductor firms.

Restoring the competitiveness of U.S. semiconductor firms will require, above all, improving production yields and product quality, and reducing the time-to-market for new products and production processes. U.S. firms now need to match the

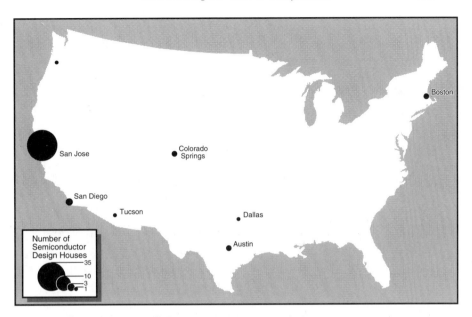

FIGURE 4.4. Location of semiconductor design-houses in the United States.

manufacturing performance of international rivals, and accelerate the transition to new products and production processes, where return on capital and R&D investment is typically higher. In practice, these two manufacturing challenges are elements of a single problem: the time involved in stabilizing new technologies on the production line and in "ramping up" to high-yield production is for many firms the major obstacle to accelerated technology development. Process control is crucial to profitability in all segments of the semiconductor industry, but especially in DRAMs, microprocessors, and other volume VLSI product markets.

Strategies for accelerated technological development are now a staple of business management analysis. Yet the concept of technology development remains poorly defined; it is typically used to describe all aspects of the manufacturing process prior to volume production of a particular product. Within this framework, most researchers continue to employ the longstanding categories of basic research, applied research, and product development. While this vocabulary is still useful, it is not conducive to a fine-grained analysis of processes of technology development, and it continues to portray technology development and production as separate (and typically sequential) aspects of the manufacturing process. This bifurcation of the manufacturing process is evident in the emphasis typically placed on product development (as opposed to improvements in process technology and production equipment) as the key element of technological change, and in the focus on engineering (as opposed to production) as the source of improvements in time-to-market for new technologies.

Analysis of technology development is complicated by the range of product and process technologies currently being used in the semiconductor industry. Each of the major product markets presents a different set of challenges for technology development. DRAMs typically involve the highest level of miniaturization; microprocessors involve a high number of steps in the manufacturing process; ASICs require the management of complex production and product variations on the manufacturing line. The elements of the technology-development process are seen most clearly, however, in the case of DRAM manufacturing. Because DRAMs are the leading production driver, improvements in production technology and manufacturing equipment typically emerge first in this product market. DRAMs also illustrate the rapid pace of new technology-development that is characteristic of semiconductor manufacturing. Figure 4.5 shows production shipments for successive generations of DRAM devices (4K, 16K, 64K, and so forth) during the period 1975–91. The cross-over time between generations of devices (i.e., the period in which a particular device accounts for the largest percentage of unit shipments) is usually less than four years. For example, 256K DRAMs emerged as the dominant device (by volume of shipments) in 1985, and were succeeded by 1M DRAMs in late 1989. Time-to-market for each generation of devices is a crucial determinant of profitability in DRAM manufacturing. The learning economies realized by firms that entered the market early, as well as the cost and time of product qualification, make it

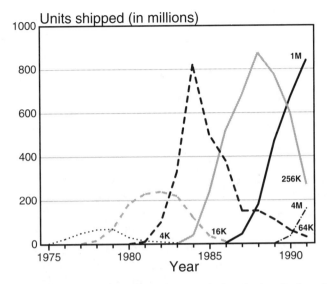

FIGURE 4.5. Shipments of DRAM integrated circuits by device density, 1975–91. (Adapted from Integrated Circuit Engineering Corporation. 1992. *Status 1992.* Scottsdale, AZ: ICE.)

difficult for late entrants to capture substantial profits in any specific generation of DRAM technology.[8]

Figure 4.6 shows in schematic form the technology-development cycle for DRAM integrated circuits.[9] Most discussions of accelerated technology development in the semiconductor and other high-technology industries focus on product development, that is, on the process whereby an idea is translated into a manufacturable product. Depending on the complexity of the product, and on the amount of new technology required, the product-development phase can last from six

---

[8]While late entrants can capture a substantial market share, this is typically achieved by discounting prices to below the actual cost of production. Many late entrants have been willing to bear such losses in order to initiate the process of "learning-by-doing," and to create the foundation for possible early-entry into the next generation of technology. Market-share strategies such as these have triggered charges of dumping against both Japanese and South Korean firms.

[9]I am grateful to Graydon Larrabee, formerly Senior Fellow at Texas Instruments, for laying out this model of the DRAM cycle.

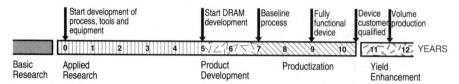

FIGURE 4.6. Technology-development cycle for DRAM integrated circuits.

months to four years. In the case of DRAMs, the elapsed time between product conceptualization and the initial production of a fully functioning device is approximately three and one-half years. As shown in Figure 4.6, however, the full technology-development cycle for DRAMs extends over more than ten years. Product development, per se, is only one element of a more complex and extensive technology-development process: prior to initial product development, semiconductor manufacturers engage in extensive research on enabling process technologies and equipment, and crucial processes of device qualification and yield enhancement follow initial product development.

The full technology-development cycle begins with basic research, which is usually conducted in universities or central research laboratories. This basic research overlaps and is succeeded by approximately five years of applied R&D, which is focused on the development of enabling process technologies, materials, and manufacturing equipment. In the case of DRAMs, much of this applied research is directed toward developing technologies and equipment necessary to achieve the greater levels of circuit integration and feature miniaturization associated with each generation of DRAM devices. Currently under development, for example, are a range of lithography, etching, and planarization technologies necessary for the manufacture of 256M devices with 0.25 micron feature sizes (production of 256M devices will not begin until the end of the 1990s). In addition, semiconductor firms and associated equipment suppliers are working to develop new systems of factory automation and computer-integrated manufacturing software and technology. Process and equipment R&D overlaps with the actual development of the DRAM device and a period known in the industry as "productization," during which a baseline technology is translated into a fully qualified device. Productization is then followed by a period of yield enhancement associated with the ramp up to volume production.

In the context of this broader conception of technology development, a task of central importance is the identification of those aspects of the manufacturing process that present the greatest opportunities for, and the greatest barriers to, reduced time-to-market for new products and production processes. What, for example, are the opportunities for shortening the time involved in developing new manufacturing equipment and enabling technologies? Can the process of applied research or product design be accelerated (in the absence of major new investments in R&D)?

In addressing these issues, semiconductor manufacturers are currently exploring various dimensions of the technology-development process. Firms with major in-house R&D activities, such as IBM and Texas Instruments, are moving toward a greater systematization of basic research, using sophisticated computer software systems to scan, monitor, store, and retrieve information from universities and research laboratories around the world. Similarly, efforts are currently underway to reduce the time involved in designing high-density integrated circuits. Major advances in this area have been made through the use of software compilers and system emulation technology. In addition, a number of firms are exploring the application of "Total Quality Management" (TQM) to research and design activities.[10] While now commonplace on the factory floor, TQM has historically been resisted by researchers and engineers who view their activities as impervious to systematization. As the complexity and scale of circuit designs have increased, however, semiconductor firms have sought ways to streamline the design process (e.g., partitioning the process in ways that minimize the amount of original software written for a new product).

---

[10]Total Quality Management involves the implementation of a range of practices (e.g., statistical process control, failure analysis, and quality enhancement teams) designed to improve manufacturing performance incrementally, and to eliminate sources of product failure, equipment downtime, and the like.

Increasing the efficiency of the circuit design process is crucial for accelerating product development, especially in ASIC and other specialized markets. Interestingly, however, the most significant progress in accelerating technology development has occurred not in the areas of research or product development, but in the final phases of productization and yield enhancement, that is, in *translating technological capability into a high-yield production process*. Historically, these later phases of the technology-development cycle have been a source of competitive weakness for U.S. firms. While Texas Instruments, for example, was one of the first firms to announce the development of a working laboratory version of a 4M DRAM, it was the Japanese firm Hitachi that was first to achieve volume production of the device. Similarly, the current struggle for market leadership in flash memory revolves not so much around product technology (which is available through licensing agreements and cooperative R&D), but around the transition to high-yield volume production of each successive generation of products. In short, production is at the core of accelerated technology development, a finding that is at odds with much of the conventional wisdom concerning the dynamics of innovation and technological change.

In recent years, U.S. manufacturers of DRAMs, SRAMs, microprocessors, and other VLSI devices have made substantial progress in productization, in stabilizing manufacturing processes on the production line, and in enhancing the yields achieved in volume production. Central to this success has been the full integration of production into the technology-development process, overcoming a previously bifurcated manufacturing form.

Integrating Production into Technology Development

Until the early 1980s, the dominant model for technology development in large U.S. semiconductors firms involved the organizational, and in most cases the geographical, separation of different phases of the manufacturing process (basic research, applied research, product development, production, marketing, and so forth). New products and production processes were passed along the technology-development chain from one facility and manufacturing group to another, from research to product development to production. Technology development under this disarticulated manufacturing form was not only time consuming, but also difficult to achieve, as conflicts and lapses in communication among the various manufacturing groups routinely delayed the introduction of new products. With the shift to devices involving higher levels of circuit integration, these difficulties were further compounded and resulted in increasingly poor yields on production lines.

Learning from their Japanese competitors, U.S. semiconductor firms moved rapidly during the mid-1980s to integrate the various stages of the technology-development cycle. To a significant degree, the attendant changes have been organizational in nature. The most important of these changes has been the creation of multidimensional technology-development teams that include personnel from internal research, product development, production, and marketing operations, as well as from external equipment and materials suppliers. These teams are formed early in the technology-development cycle and follow products through to final production. A primary responsibility of the team is to introduce the concerns of production and marketing at the beginning of the technology-development cycle, thus shifting technology development away from its heretofore central focus on innovation and toward the creation of a manufacturable and a sellable product.

The precise form of these development teams varies among semiconductor firms. The teams are most prevalent in large firms, where problems of communication among different manufacturing groups are especially intense; the small size of start-up firms facilitates more informal communication and provides for less organizational separation of the different phases of technology development.[11]

The technology-development teams at IBM are typical of those at large semiconductor manufacturers. In mid-1988,

[11]It is important to note in this regard that many start-up firms use external foundries for wafer fabrication. The effects of production subcontracting and other forms of interorganizational linkage on manufacturing performance are examined in Chapter 5.

IBM formed a series of internal organizational units charged with the task of facilitating and coordinating the activities of research, product development, production, marketing, and other aspects of the manufacturing process. While labelled "advanced technology laboratories" (e.g., the Advanced Semiconductor Technology Laboratory and the Advanced Packaging Technology Laboratory), these units are only nominal organizations; their members are based in other units of the company and meet on a regular basis to manage and coordinate the technology-development process. In addition to IBM's internal staff, representatives of external vendors and equipment suppliers also participate in the technology laboratories.

Product-development teams such as those at IBM, as well as similar organizational innovations, are now commonplace in high-technology firms. What is interesting and unique about these innovations in the semiconductor industry is that the integration of production into the technological development process has gone beyond mere organizational form, involving the physical and geographical integration of innovation and production. Product development, pilot production, and volume production now occur in the same technology-development facility, rather than in a series of separate, dedicated manufacturing plants. This movement from organizational to geographical integration has been driven by the immense difficulties experienced in stabilizing manufacturing processes on the production line; by using the same facility, semiconductor manufacturers are able to avoid bringing up manufacturing processes sequentially in research, pilot production, and volume production facilities, thereby reducing dramatically the time required to reach volume production and improving the yields achieved on the production line.

Borrowing the terminology used by Intel Corporation, one of the pioneers in moving beyond the traditional disarticulated manufacturing form, the present study refers to these new integrated plants as "development facilities." Until the early 1980s, Intel operated its fabrication facilities as stand-alone production plants under the control of the manufacturing branch of the company (as opposed to the engineering branch or any of the product technology groups). In the early 1980s, the company began to integrate production into technology development, adding a technology development annex to each of its wafer fabrication plants.[12] This intermediate step failed, however, to secure the desired integration of innovation and production within the overall technology-development cycle. In the mid-1980s, Intel constructed its first, fully integrated development facility alongside its corporate headquarters in Santa Clara; a second development facility was subsequently added in Hillsboro, Oregon. These facilities serve as the primary centers of semiconductor technology development for the company, integrating process and equipment development, product development, productization, and yield enhancement (see Figure 4.7).

Development facilities are rapidly emerging as the central venue for the technology development activities of large U.S. semiconductor firms. Most of the major U.S. merchant producers (Advanced Micro Devices, Intel, Motorola, Texas Instruments) operate one or more development facilities, as do several smaller leading-edge firms (e.g., Integrated Device Technology and VLSI Technology). The precise form of the facilities varies among firms. At IBM, where the facilities are called Early Production Lines (EPLs), the focus is on stabilizing production processes prior to transferring them to other high-volume production lines. In introducing EPLs in the late 1980s, IBM actually eliminated the pilot production phase of the manufacturing process by conducting pilot production on the development lines.

Texas Instruments has taken the concept of development facilities the furthest among U.S. semiconductor firms. The immediate stimulus for integrated product development and production came from the relatively weak performance of Texas Instruments in 4M DRAMs. Although DRAM development at Texas Instruments is based on a technology-development alliance with Hitachi of Japan, the two companies have used different product designs in 4M and 16M DRAMs. Texas Instruments designed and developed its 4M DRAM de-

---

[12]This intermediate manufacturing form is akin to what Glasmeier (1988) has described as a technical branch plant.

vice at its research facilities in Dallas, and then "passed over" the product to its manufacturing plant in Miho, Japan. The time involved in bringing up the product at the Miho facility delayed Texas Instrument's entry into the marketplace; Hitachi, by contrast, was first among all international competitors in achieving volume production. Learning from this experience, Texas Instruments chose to manufacture the next generation of 16M DRAMs at an integrated development facility in Dallas; both product development and production were conducted at the same plant, and the same engineering team was kept on the project from research through product qualification to volume production. Texas Instruments's 64M devices will be built at a parallel development facility in Japan.

In addition to creating integrated development facilities, Texas Instruments has reconfigured the relations among its manufacturing plants around the world. Like most major semiconductor manufacturers, Texas Instruments maintains volume wafer-fabrication capacity in Europe (Avezzano, Italy) and in Southeast Asia (Taiwan). The latter manufacturing facility is a joint venture with Acer, a major Taiwanese computer manufacturer. In the past, the European and Asian facilities have been brought on-line mid-way through the product cycle, providing additional high-volume capacity for mature products developed in the United States. As in the initial transition from pilot production to volume production, considerable difficulty was often experienced in bringing new processes on-line at the European and Asian facilities. One of the major obstacles involved differences in the production equipment and materials used in U.S. and offshore facilities; production processes often had to be restabilized on the new production lines. In response to these difficulties, Texas Instruments has moved to standardize its manufacturing capability worldwide by establishing a series of parallel facilities using standard equipment and manufacturing procedures (a process Texas Instruments calls "harmonization"). Equipment procurement decisions for all manufacturing plants throughout the world are now made at the initial development facility. At the same time, the engineering staff responsible for bringing a product on-line at the original development facility (in Dallas, Texas, or Miho, Japan) also serves as a transfer team responsible for establishing the process at facilities around the world. As a result of these changes, Texas Instruments has dramatically reduced the time required to establish volume manufacturing capability around the globe, and has improved the manufacturing performance of its fabrication plants throughout the world.

Development facilities mark a substantial break with the traditional organizational and geographical division of labor in technology development. Figure 4.7 shows in schematic form the changes in the network of semiconductor manufacturing plants. Under the previously dominant manufacturing model, semiconductor firms maintained a network of product de-velopment, pilot production, and volume production facilities, each of which specialized in one element of the technology-development process. Technology and ideas were passed from one facility to another (oftentimes located in different regions of the United States), and from one manufacturing group to another, as a product moved through the technology-develop-ment cycle. Under the new manufacturing model, all aspects of fabrication technology development, beyond basic research, are centralized at integrated technology-development facilities, which then transfer technology to parallel production facilities in each of the major continental trading areas (Asia, Europe,

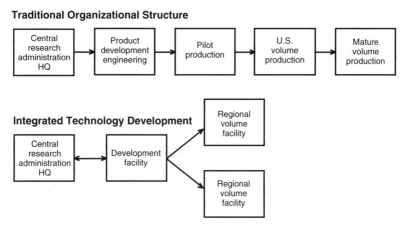

FIGURE 4.7. The changing structure of technology development.

and North America). Organizational and geographical disarticulation is giving way to a global network of integrated development facilities.

One consequence of the movement to integrated development facilities has been a resurgence of manufacturing investment in Silicon Valley and other major centers of technology development. In the face of an ongoing trend to geographically disperse high-volume production away from Silicon Valley, many analysts anticipated a deepening spatial division of labor, in which Silicon Valley would retain its role as a center of research and product design but lose most of its production operations. Among the major merchant semiconductor manufacturers, however, Advanced Micro Devices, Intel, and Signetics have located new integrated-development facilities in the region. Intel Corporation has recently announced a further $400 million expansion of its Silicon Valley development facility; the plant will soon provide the most advanced (0.5 microns) production capability of any maintained by the company in the world. Silicon Valley is becoming not so much a traditional center of R&D (with few production workers), but an integrated center of advanced technology development that anchors a network of volume production facilities in global markets, and routinized assembly facilities at low-wage locations in the world's semiperiphery.

Concurrent Engineering

Integration of production into the technology-development process is having a substantial impact on time-to-market in the semiconductor industry. There are limits, however, to the opportunities firms have to shorten the technology-development cycle on any particular product. Efforts to shorten such cycles for individual products have been accompanied, therefore, by a shift toward a system of concurrent engineering.

Concurrent engineering is a general term that refers to the simultaneous rather than the sequential development of allied technologies. In its most direct form, concurrent engineering involves the development of several different generations of product technology at one time. Figure 4.8 illustrates the practice for the case of DRAM integrated circuits. At the present time, most manufacturers have three generations of DRAM circuits in various stages of development (16M in productization, 64M in product development, and 256M in applied research). Two additional generations (4M and 1M) are in volume production. Previously, it was commonplace for semiconductor firms and other high-technology manufacturers to complete the development of one product before initiating the development of next-generation technology. As shown in Figure 4.8, however, DRAM manufacturers now initiate development of next-generation products even before the latest technology has been qualified for use by customers.

Parallel product development is only one aspect of concurrent engineering. The term also refers to the simultaneous development of component and system-level technology, of software and hardware technology, and of products and production equipment. The development of new microprocessor technologies, for example, now takes place in tandem with the development of computers that incorporate the technology,

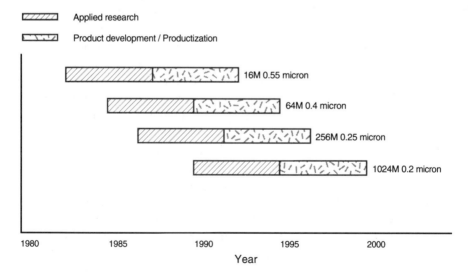

FIGURE 4.8. Concurrent engineering of DRAM integrated circuits.

allowing manufacturers to introduce new products within days of the first production of the new microprocessor.[13] Similarly, manufacturers of testing equipment are already developing systems to meet the demands of next-generation semiconductor technologies.

For parallel product development to be sustained over more than a brief period of time, it is necessary for firms to codevelop manufacturing capability and market demand. In the absence of such activity, the development of new generations of products becomes constrained by the limits of older process equipment, and by the ability of firms to design new high-density semiconductors into electronic systems. This is currently an issue of major concern within the U.S. semiconductor industry. Many believe that, in the absence of substantial additional R&D funding for process and equipment development, product development will be constrained by the end of the 1990s, creating market opportunities for foreign competitors.

Overlapping technology-development cycles are becoming increasingly common in the semiconductor industry and can have a substantial impact on the elapsed time between each generation of product technology. Intel Corporation, for example, estimates that shifting to concurrent technology development will cut the elapsed time between generations of microprocessors in half, from three years to one and one-half years. At the same time, however, the difficulties involved in sustaining such a rate of product development are immense. Of immediate significance is the large increase in R&D expenditures required to support multiple projects at the same time. When Intel shifted to concurrent development of microprocessors in mid-1990, the company simultaneously announced a large increase in R&D and capital expenditures. After raising its capital and R&D expenditures to $1.5 billion in 1991, Intel announced a further round of increases and expected to spend in excess of $2 billion in capital and R&D investments in 1992 (of which approximately $800 million was for R&D). With

---

[13]This strategy gained widespread publicity when Compaq beat out its competitors in introducing a personal computer based on Intel's 80286 microprocessor.

semiconductor firms already spending as much as 20% of their revenue on R&D, the increase in R&D expenditures required for overlapping technology development cycles is difficult to sustain, leading many firms to join together in technology-development partnerships.

More generally, concurrent engineering requires fundamental changes in existing manufacturing practice. Above all, it requires extensive communication between semiconductor manufacturers, customers, and equipment suppliers concerning the anticipated characteristics of next-generation technologies. Computer manufacturers, for example, need to know the performance characteristics, power dissipation requirements, packaging format, and many other features of technologies that are still in development. Customers must design the technologies into their products before the technologies are produced in volume. At the same time, equipment manufacturers need to anticipate the process requirements for next generation technologies. In short, concurrent engineering requires tighter bonds and increased communication among customers, semiconductor producers, and suppliers. The most important of these linkages are those between semiconductor producers and equipment suppliers.

Equipment Suppliers

The rapid development and deployment of leading-edge fabrication equipment is central to the efforts of U.S. semiconductor firms to improve manufacturing performance and reduce time-to-market on new products and production processes. As previously shown in Figure 4.6, the development of next generation fabrication technology is a key element of the overall technology-development cycle for DRAMs and other advanced semiconductor devices. While semiconductor manufacturers have in the past developed fabrication equipment in-house, most firms now purchase the technology from external vendors. The shift to concurrent engineering, accelerated product development, and higher production yields has placed a premium on close contacts between semiconductor manufacturers and external equipment suppliers.

For much of the 1980s, the relations between U.S. firms and domestic equipment suppliers were notoriously poor (see Chapter 2). A recent survey by the U.S. General Accounting Office (1990) only underscored the ineffective working relationship between manufacturers and suppliers in the U.S. semiconductor industry. Of thirty-one equipment suppliers questioned in the survey, twenty-three (74.2%) reported that semiconductor manufacturers did not include them in their planning activities, and twenty-one (67.7%) reported that relations were based on purely short-term considerations and did not involve the sharing of key technical data concerning the performance of manufacturing equipment (e.g., yields achieved in production). The experience of Japan, by contrast, demonstrated that "thick line" relations between semiconductor producers and equipment suppliers can have a substantially positive impact on manufacturing performance. Drawing on the Japanese model, many U.S. semiconductor manufacturers in the late 1980s began to establish closer ties with equipment suppliers.

Data collected in the questionnaire survey administered for the present study allow for a preliminary evaluation of the nature and extent of changing producer–supplier linkages in the U.S. semiconductor industry. Of the seventy-two firms in the survey sample, forty-eight (66.7%) operate one or more wafer fabrication facilities; the latter subsample of firms was asked to provide a variety of information on relations with equipment suppliers. As indicated above, the drive to improve manufacturing yields and to accelerate technology development emphasizes extensive interaction and exchange of information between semiconductor producers and suppliers. For the purposes of the present analysis, data were obtained on five types of producer–supplier interaction: (a) institution of a formal program to evaluate suppliers; (b) institution of a partnership program with suppliers; (c) use of wafer fabrication facilities as test sites for supplier equipment; (d) sharing of technical information with suppliers (e.g., yield rates achieved on equipment); and (e) cooperation with suppliers on technology development. Supplier-evaluation programs are systems for formally evaluating supplier performance; such programs have

TABLE 4.2. Relationships between Semiconductor Firms and Equipment Suppliers

	Percentage of survey sample engaged in activity
Formal evaluation of suppliers	29.2
Partnership program with suppliers	22.9
Use of firm as a test site by suppliers	31.2
Exchange of technical information with suppliers	56.2
Cooperative technology-development agreements with suppliers	16.7

$n = 48$.

become a key element of quality-enhancement strategies in the semiconductor and other high-technology manufacturing industries. Partnership programs involve the designation of a small set of preferred suppliers (or partners) who work most closely with manufacturers and who typically receive a high proportion of orders for production equipment.

Table 4.2 shows the percentage of the sampled semiconductor firms that engage in one or more of these five types of producer–supplier interaction. Only one type of interaction (exchange of technical information) is engaged in by a majority of the sampled firms. Of the forty-eight firms in the sample, twenty-seven (56.2%) indicated that they routinely share technical information with their equipment suppliers. While many semiconduction firms still do not share technical data with suppliers, the findings of the present survey suggest some improvement relative to the findings of a survey conducted by the General Accounting Office (1990) some two years earlier.[14] With regard to the other types of supplier interaction, however, the survey indicates that only a minority of the sampled firms have established close relations with equipment suppliers.

---

[14]It is important to note in this regard that the GAO surveyed equipment suppliers rather than semiconductor firms. To some extent, the lower level of information exchange reported in the GAO survey reflects the different perceptions of semiconductor manufacturers and equipment suppliers regarding an appropriate level of information exchange.

Fourteen firms (29.2%) maintain a formal program to evaluate suppliers; eleven firms (22.9%) have established partnership programs with suppliers; and eight firms (16.6%) have signed a cooperative technology-development agreement with one or more equipment suppliers. By way of comparison, a parallel study of the relations between semiconductor firms and their *customers* found that 52.1% of the customers' firms maintain a formal program to evaluate semiconductor manufacturers, 38.0% maintain a partnership program, and 31.9% a technology-development agreement (Angel in press). Semiconductor firms apparently lag behind their customers in recognizing the need for close relations with suppliers.

These findings suggest that, pressures to improve manufacturing performance notwithstanding, only a minority of U.S. semiconductor firms have substantially restructured their relations with equipment suppliers. Follow-up interviews with the semiconductor firms that were initially sampled, however, indicate a more complex picture. First, as shown in Figure 4.9, most of the evaluation and partnership programs are of recent origin. In the case of IBM, for example, a substantial restructuring of the procurement procedures for semiconductor equipment was initiated at the end of 1989, in conjunction with the establishment of a Strategic Equipment Council responsible

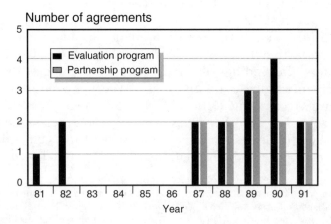

FIGURE 4.9. Date of initiation of supplier evaluation and partnership programs.

for all purchasing decisions for semiconductor equipment. As the effects of supplier partnerships become evident to the industry as a whole, it is likely that more firms will move to establish such programs.

Second, the significance of maintaining close relations with equipment suppliers varies with the sophistication of the process technology used by semiconductor firms. Close relations are of greatest importance for firms that use leading-edge fabrication equipment (e.g., manufacturers of DRAMs and other high-density submicron products). By contrast, many firms actually use mature, second-generation manufacturing equipment that is often bought secondhand from the major merchant semiconductor manufacturers. Among firms using leading-edge technology, the movement toward close relations with equipment suppliers is substantial. All first-tier merchant and captive semiconductor manufacturers have established evaluation and partnership programs.[15] Typically these partnerships involve the use of manufacturing facilities as test sites for equipment, as well as the exchange of information on the performance of equipment under actual manufacturing conditions. The semiconductor firms that were interviewed reported substantial positive benefits from partnerships with equipment suppliers.

One of the major criticisms of U.S. semiconductor firms is that they have tended to shift the cost and the risk of new technology development onto equipment manufacturers. Rising equipment costs, however, are making it increasingly difficult for small equipment manufacturers to sustain the necessary R&D investments. Many analysts have argued that U.S. semiconductor firms should follow the Japanese example and enter into cooperative technology-development agreements with equipment manufacturers (Stowsky 1989). As shown in Table 4.2, only a minority of U.S. semiconductor firms have as yet followed this path. Among such firms, IBM has gone the

---

[15]Sematech has played a key mediating role in this regard. The fourteen founding members of Sematech participate in a Sematech program, known as Partnering for Total Quality, that has done much to promote closer relations between U.S. semiconductor producers and equipment suppliers. The contribution of Sematech and other government programs is discussed in detail in Chapter 6.

furthest in conducting joint technology development with equipment suppliers. The company currently has technology development agreements with numerous suppliers, including Applied Materials, Eteq, KLA Instruments, Lam Research, Micrion, and the lithography division of Silicon Valley Group.

Bilateral technology development agreements, however, present a number of difficulties for both semiconductor firms and equipment suppliers. First, the tendency in many bilateral agreements has been to development equipment that is fine-tuned to the needs of the partner semiconductor firm. Rather than developing generic technology, partnerships programs and technology development agreements tend to focus on the performance of equipment under specific process and manufacturing conditions. As a result, bilateral partnerships have a reduced impact on the competitive prospects of equipment suppliers. Second, joint technology agreements often lead to serious problems concerning the ownership of the resultant technology. While the semiconductor firm typically wishes to retain proprietary control over equipment developed in the partnership, the equipment manufacturer wishes to maximize the return on its R&D investments through open-market sales to other semiconductor firms.

The problem of proprietorship, and the possibility of free rider activity, explain in part the relatively small number of bilateral technology partnerships established between U.S. semiconductor firms and their equipment suppliers. As I discuss in detail in Chapter 6, industry consortia have proven to be a useful alternative organizational form for facilitating cooperative R&D between semiconductor manufacturers and equipment suppliers.

CONCLUSION

The changes described in this chapter constitute nothing less than a fundamental remaking of manufacturing practice in the U.S. semiconductor industry. Integration of production into the technology-development process, and of suppliers and customers into the operations of semiconductor firms, removes major longstanding barriers to improved manufacturing performance in the U.S. semiconductor industry. While organizational and geographical restructuring are still of recent origin (dating primarily from the late 1980s), their effects are already visible in improved production yields, higher product quality, and accelerated rates of product and process technology development. Continuation of the current trend in restructuring, and the diffusion of new manufacturing practices throughout the U.S. semiconductor industry, will make a major contribution to the stabilization of U.S. market share in semiconductors during the 1990s.

It is important to note that organizational and geographical restructuring only create the framework within which internationally competitive standards of manufacturing performance can be achieved. In the end, world-class manufacturing presumes the existence of necessary skills and capabilities among workers and management, and the maintenance of a system of employment relations that supports continuous improvement in production. Of particular significance in this regard has been the implementation by many semiconductor firms of various formal and informal quality-improvement programs that, once again, are modeled on manufacturing practices successfully maintained by Japanese semiconductor firms. These programs, which are widely discussed in the literature, involve the introduction of quality-control teams, the increased use of statistical process control, and other forms of reliability and failure analysis. Organizational and geographical restructuring have created the conditions under which these micropractices can have a substantial impact on manufacturing performance.

CHAPTER 5

Global and Local Partnerships

Efforts to enhance the competitiveness of U.S. semiconductor firms have occurred at a time of significant change in product and process technologies. The movement to higher levels of circuit integration, to submicron fabrication, and to new Application Specific Integrated Circuit (ASIC) and Computer Automated Design (CAD) technologies has fundamentally altered the existing structure of economies of scale and scope in semiconductor manufacturing and triggered important changes in the organizational structure of the industry. This chapter explores the major dimensions of change in organizational form, focusing on the proliferation of cooperative agreements and technology partnerships among semiconductor firms. Whether they are start-up ventures or large corporations, few semiconductor firms stand alone: the majority are now enmeshed in a complex network of research, technology development, production, and marketing alliances.

The chapter begins with an overview of the processes underlying the spread of alliances involving U.S. semiconductor firms. I then examine in detail the nature and extent of these interfirm alliances and consider the likely effects of this emergent organizational structure on regional economic development in the United States. Many alliances are international in scope, raising fears of an accelerated diffusion of technology to foreign competitors, and of intensified instability and job loss in U.S. high-technology production complexes. The present analysis suggests, however, that participation in the emergent global network of alliances can have a positive impact on employment in high-technology industries in the United States.

THE FORMATION OF INTERFIRM PARTNERSHIPS

The sources of the most recent phase of organizational restructuring in the semiconductor industry are complex, involving a variety of intersecting changes in technology, markets, and manufacturing processes. However, the shift to higher levels of circuit integration, and to submicron levels of device fabrication, has been of central importance. Over the past decade, semiconductor manufacturing has become dominated by VLSI (very large-scale integration) technologies that combine thousands of electronic functions at microscopic scale on a single chip. The twin processes of circuit integration and miniaturization have strengthened two important incentives for organizational change. The first is increased pressure on semiconductor firms to share the expense and risk of rapidly growing investments in R&D, facilities, and equipment. The second is the tendency toward greater design and market specialization on the part of semiconductor firms. Jointly, these two incentives explain in large part the formation of partnerships among firms possessing complementary manufacturing expertise and market specialization.

Sharing Risks and Costs

The key technological and manufacturing development underlying the formation of interfirm partnerships has been the shift to VLSI production and submicron fabrication. This shift has led, in turn, to a rapid increase in the costs of R&D, equipment, and facilities. R&D costs for the next generation of DRAM integrated circuits are expected to exceed $1 billion. The cost of a leading-edge, high-volume fabrication facility has approximately tripled during the 1980s, rising to more than $600 million. Individual pieces of manufacturing equipment, such as lithography systems, can cost in excess of $3 million. While scaled-down "mini-fabs" are less expensive (approximately $100 million), even their cost is prohibitive for smaller firms and start-up companies.

As the costs of R&D, equipment, and facilities have increased, so has the risk to firms of market failure; the inability of a firm to gain market acceptance of new product lines leaves production capacity idle and provides little return on R&D investments, thus undermining the profitability of even very large firms. In response to these changing technological and economic conditions, many semiconductor firms have sought ways to share the risks and costs of up-front investments in process technology and production facilities. In general, this has involved the establishment of manufacturing agreements with other semiconductor firms. In the case of design houses, the costs of production are shared through the use of outside foundries that pool the production requirements of several houses to achieve efficient levels of capacity utilization. In the case of larger, integrated semiconductor firms, the risks and costs of semiconductor manufacturing are shared through the joint development and production of new process and product technologies.

Market and Technology Specialization

The second key development underlying the proliferation of alliances involving U.S. semiconductor firms is the trend toward increased market and technology specialization. The majority of these alliances involve producers that specialize in different markets, technologies, or stages of the manufacturing process (e.g., product versus process technology).

Specialization has been encouraged by the widespread shift to higher levels of circuit integration, and by the falling costs of integrated-circuit design associated with ASIC and CAD technologies. At high levels of circuit integration, semiconductor devices are able to incorporate multiple device functions and to provide, on a single chip, much of the logic circuitry of a complete electronic system. The value of the device is closely linked to the efficiency of the design in meeting customer needs; consequently, semiconductor firms have had to become much more familiar with the system characteristics of different markets, and to develop expertise in particular market segments. In response to these technological developments, the focus of semiconductor manufacturing has been shifting away from the longstanding emphasis on standard components, and toward the custom designing of high-integration

ASIC and Application Specific Standard Products (ASSP) devices for particular market segments. While the market share of standard components, such as DRAMs and other memory devices, remains large, the highest rates of return are now obtained on investments in design-intensive products. Generic expertise in semiconductor production and process technology is giving way to specialized expertise in particular product technologies and markets.

As the shift away from standard components has occurred, a form of market fragmentation has taken place, with semiconductor firms developing specialized design expertise in different markets segments and niches, such as telecommunications or computers. Relative to the proliferation of different market segments, the expertise of individual firms is increasingly circumscribed within particular product areas and geographical markets. The actual pattern of market segmentation is one of some complexity. There remain important economies of scope across many products; experience gained in developing microcontrollers for computer equipment, for example, is transferable to other markets, such as emissions-control devices in automobiles. Manufacturing expertise is only rarely limited to one specific product, and there are many broadly based semiconductor firms operating in multiple market niches. Even large firms, however, are limited in their ability to develop requisite expertise and experience in all market segments and geographical market areas.

The constraints on firms reflect in part the varied design environments associated with different markets, and the need to develop very close contacts with customers in each market area—contacts that support synergistic learning and the transfer of knowledge between the customer and the supplier of semiconductors. The constraints also reflect the different product-design requirements in the major international trading blocks of North America, Asia, and Europe. The design expertise gained in serving U.S. customers is often not directly transferable to the Japanese or European markets. Moreover, many U.S. firms have great difficulty establishing the market contacts in Japan and Europe that are needed to develop effective design solutions for these markets. As a result, it has be-

come increasingly difficult even for large, global firms to remain on the leading-edge in all product markets and geographical market areas.

The increased emphasis on design expertise has provided
new openings for start-up firms in the semiconductor industry.
Most new ventures specialize in particular product technologies
and market niches, drawing on their knowledge of, and expertise in, a limited market area to provide high-quality circuit
designs. In the majority of cases, these firms are actually design
houses that subcontract out the production and assembly stages
of the manufacturing process. Small design houses represent in
many ways the extreme case of market and technology specialization. As indicated above, however, the tendency to specialize
is also evident among larger firms. Unlike the smaller start-up
firms, the larger firms have not narrowed their product lines.
Indeed, the reverse is true: most large firms now manufacture
a greater variety of products than in the past. However, the
variety of product markets and geographical market areas has
increased rapidly, leaving even large firms with competency in
only a few markets.

Semiconductor manufacturers throughout the world have
responded to these developments by forming partnerships with
producers possessing complementary marketing and technological expertise. Such partnerships are an organizational
form that combines specialized market and product competencies with more generic technological and production
capabilities in order to minimize the production costs of providing new technological solutions to diverse market segments. As
I discuss below, the fact that firms possess different specialized
expertise is both a motivation for partnership and a key determinant of the durability of the relationship.

Making Partnerships Work

While the need to share costs and risks is a powerful incentive
for the formation of alliances, partnering with outside manufacturers presents substantial risks for semiconductor firms.
Specifically, the question arises as to how the partner firms can
avoid free-rider problems and exercise proprietary control

over the knowledge generated by the partnership. As technology and ideas are transferred from one partner to another, collaborators rapidly become competitors, and the alliance collapses. The recent history of the semiconductor industry is replete with examples of this scenario. Many of the partnerships formed between U.S. design houses and Japanese manufacturers, for example, have created additional competition in low end ASICs and other markets once dominated by U.S. firms. Similar problems have emerged in alliances among U.S. firms, such as the technology partnership between Xilinx and AT&T for the development and marketing of gate arrays.[1] Williamson (1985) and others have argued that the problems of appropriability and knowledge protection are powerful incentives for vertical integration of design and production.

Parkhe (1993) suggests that the key analytical issues for the partners are trust, reciprocity, and forbearance. Under what conditions will partner firms place the stability of the partnership ahead of any gains to be had from violating the terms and spirit of an agreement? Trust and goodwill are apparently not enough. Partnerships have to be structured so that the opportunities for, and gains from, malfeasance are outweighed by the benefits of continuing the alliance.

In principle, the extent of any right to use technology can be fully specified in the contractual agreement between partner firms. The experience of U.S. semiconductor firms suggests, however, that the property rights included in contractual agreements need to be safeguarded by additional conditions that prevent collaborators from becoming competitors. Of particular importance in this regard is the identification of so-called complementary assets that remain the exclusive property of each partner firm. To the extent that knowledge developed jointly within an alliance must be combined in the manufacturing process with complementary assets or expertise, each partner maintains a distinct area of competitive advantage. Generic

---

[1] In this partnership, Xilinx licensed AT&T to manufacture and sell elements of its line of Field Programmable Gate Arrays, in an apparent attempt to gain wider market acceptance of its product architecture. The alliance turned sour when AT&T began to cut prices on the products, reducing Xilinx's profits and market share. It is now unlikely that Xilinx will extend the alliance to next-generation technology.

expertise in process technology, for example, can be combined with specialized expertise in different product technologies to encourage cooperation rather than competition among partner firms. In this case, contractual disagreement is avoided through the selection of partners that possess different market and technology specializations. Jorde and Teece (1990, p. 83) make a similar argument:

> Thus a single firm or even a consortium with good intellectual property protection will often need to bolster its market position and its stream of rents by other strategies and mechanisms. These mechanisms include building, acquiring, or renting (on an exclusive basis) complementary assets and exploiting first-mover advantages. We use the term complementary assets to refer to those assets and capabilities that need to be employed to package new technology so that it is valuable to the end user. Broad categories of complementary assets include complementary technologies, manufacturing, marketing, distribution, sales, and service.

In the case of the semiconductor industry, the most significant alliances involve the codevelopment of process technologies. Knowledge regarding process technology, jointly developed within the alliance, is combined with the different specialized market and product technology assets and expertises of each of the partner firms. Some alliances involve different product markets; jointly developed process technology is used by one partner firm in the manufacture of memory circuits, and by another for the manufacture of microprocessors. Alternatively, the partners may specialize in different geographic markets; one partner sells primarily in Japan, another in the United States, both drawing on established customer linkages that are hard for the another to replicate.

Figure 5.1 illustrates in schematic form the different types of manufacturing competence and market specialization that are characteristic of the industry. Three broad areas of competence can be identified, namely, product technology, production/process technology, and geographic market. For many small firms, partnership agreements involve different areas of competence, such as product technology and process technology. For large firms, the most common type of alliance involves

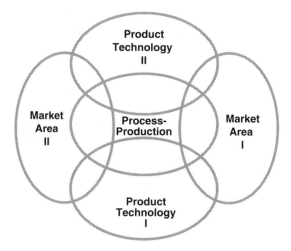

FIGURE 5.1. Sources of manufacturing advantage.

the joint development of process technology or production capability, which is combined with specialized expertise in a particular product technology or market area.

INTERFIRM AGREEMENTS: AN EMPIRICAL ANALYSIS

The structure of alliances and partnership agreements among semiconductor firms is complex. In what follows, I present empirical data on the nature and extent of cooperative activity. The sources for the data are the questionnaire survey and personal interviews described in the Appendix. Recall that the survey sample comprised seventy-two firms, of which twenty-four (33.3%) are design houses that subcontract out all wafer fabrication, and forty-eight (66.7%) are firms that operate one or more wafer fabrication facilities. The questionnaire survey obtained information on the level and type of participation in a broad range of partnerships and alliances.

"Strategic alliance" and "manufacturing partnership" are ill-defined concepts that are applied in the literature to a wide variety of formal and informal cooperative relations. What makes an alliance different from a market transaction is far from clear. At the same time, there is little agreement on what constitutes the "strategic" component of alliances. Are all alliances strategic? In its most general form, a strategic alliance is a bilateral or multilateral agreement among firms, involving cooperation in some aspect of research, technology development, production, or marketing. Such alliances include joint ventures, technology development agreements, research consortia, and production agreements. Alliances are strategic, as opposed to opportunistic, if the organizational forms of partner firms are predicated on the existence of alliances. To a significant degree, for example, the trends toward increased market specialization and vertical disintegration in the semiconductor industry presuppose the ability of semiconductor manufacturers to form partnerships with firms possessing complementary expertise.

Agreements among semiconductor firms have been a feature of the semiconductor industry since its inception. Until the early 1980s, however, these agreements were ancillary features of a pattern of industrialization centered on the individual firm. Two types of agreements were especially common in the 1960s and 1970s: patent cross-licensing and second-source agreements. The latter are agreements whereby a firm serves as a second source of supply for products developed and designed by another semiconductor company. Major end-users of high-volume products typically require a second source as protection against capacity shortfalls or manufacturing problems at the original device-manufacturer. In addition to licensing and second-source agreements, semiconductor manufacturers entered into a series of market relations with dependent subcontractors and suppliers. Perhaps the most significant of these subcontracting arrangements has been the widespread use of offshore subcontractors for device assembly. None of these arrangements altered the fundamental commitment of U.S. semiconductor firms to in-house R&D as the primary vehicle for developing new products and processes, and to vertically integrated production facilities as the primary manufacturers of semiconductor devices.

From the early 1980s onward, the organization of the manufacturing systems of many U.S. semiconductor firms began to change rapidly. The central axis of change involved an externalization of production and technology development activities, and a proliferation of cooperative agreements among semiconductor firms. By one account (Kogut and Kim 1991), more than 1,000 agreements were announced in the 1980s alone. Agreements among firms now address all types of manufacturing activities, from marketing to research and production. At the same time, there is considerable variation in the level of interaction and mutual commitment involved in these agreements, ranging from arms-length, one-time transactions, to long-term partnerships.

The focus here is on formal agreements among firms. For present purposes, we can usefully distinguish between two broad groups of agreements, based on the degree of interaction between, and the mutual commitment of, the firms involved. The first group, characterized by lower levels of interaction and commitment, includes (a) patent-licensing agreements; (b) second-sourcing agreements; (c) marketing and distribution agreements (involving the use of the sales infrastructure of another semiconductor firm to market products); and (d) investment agreements (those limited to a financial transaction only). All such agreements are administrative in character and, once established, do not usually require continuous, detailed communication among the partner firms. Marketing agreements and financial investment agreements had a large increase in frequency during the 1980s. The proliferation of marketing agreements has been closely associated with the globalization of demand for semiconductor products, and with the difficulty many firms have experienced in selling products in foreign markets. In an effort to increase global sales, U.S. firms have signed agreements with Japanese and European manufacturers to sell and distribute products in these manufacturers' domestic markets. The increase in financial investment agreements during the 1980s reflected a growing amount of Japanese and European investment in the U.S. semiconductor industry.

The second group of agreements is characterized by a higher level of interaction and commitment among the partner firms. This group includes four major types of agreements: (a) fabrication agreements; (b) technology-licensing agreements;

(c) cooperative research and technology-development agreements; and (d) manufacturing joint-venture agreements. Fabrication agreements are defined as arrangements whereby one semiconductor firm subcontracts out all or part of its device-fabrication to another semiconductor manufacturer. Most semiconductor firms subcontract out a proportion of their fabrication work; design houses subcontract out all of their device-fabrication work. In some cases, the fabrication agreement is a simple "foundry" arrangement that does not involve any transfer of the right to use or sell product technology to the subcontractor. It is often the case, however, that the fabrication arrangement is accompanied by a technology-licensing agreement under which the subcontractor gains the right to manufacture and sell products using the prime contractor's technology. In the present analysis, an important distinction is made between technology licensing agreements and the more commonplace patent licensing arrangements. As defined here, technology licensing involves the direct and active transfer of technology from one firm to another, whether in the form of a process technology "recipe," a circuit schematic, a microcode, or design software. Patent licensing, by contrast, is an administrative practice that allows a firm to gain compensation when its proprietary technology is used by another manufacturer.

The final two types of agreements—cooperative technology-development agreements and manufacturing joint-venture agreements—involve the highest level of interaction among semiconductor firms. Cooperative technology development includes basic and applied research and as well as joint development of new products and production processes. Manufacturing joint ventures are jointly owned and operated production facilities.

In the questionnaire survey, semiconductor firms were asked to list their participation in the four types of "high interaction" agreements. Table 5.1 shows the average number of active agreements of each type in which the sampled firms participated in 1990. Data are provided for all firms and for two subsamples, namely, vertically disintegrated design houses and firms with in-house fabrication capability. Some further clarification of these data is in order. First, because the data

TABLE 5.1. Average Number of High-Interaction Agreements for Sampled Semiconductor Firms, 1990

Type of agreement	Design houses	Fabrication firms	All firms
Fabrication (foundry)	1.9	0.9	1.2
Technology licensing	1.2	2.3	2.0
Cooperative technology development	0.6	1.7	1.3
Manufacturing joint venture	0.0	0.2	0.1
Total number of agreements	3.7	5.1	4.6
Number of firms	24	48	72

refer to agreements rather than alliances, the totals are not directly comparable to a count of strategic alliances. A single alliance (such as that between VLSI Technology and the Japanese firm Hitachi) often contains several agreements (e.g., one agreement to license current technology and a second agreement to cooperate on future product development). In the present analysis, each agreement is counted separately, thereby allowing a finer-grained examination of interfirm relations. Second, firms were asked to include all active agreements, whether they were the supplier or the recipient of technology, service, or production activity. In the case of technology licensing, for example, firms were asked to count agreements under which they license technology to or from another semiconductor firm. Lastly, it is important to reemphasize that the data shown in Table 5.1 refer to "high interaction" agreements only, and that the total number of agreements (including patent cross licensing, marketing, investment, and so forth) is substantially larger.

The twenty-four design houses in the survey sample maintain an average of 3.7 high-interaction agreements with other semiconductor firms, comprising an average of 1.9 foundry agreements for the provision of fabrication services, 1.2 technology-licensing agreements, and 0.6 cooperative technology-development agreements. By definition, design houses lack in-house fabrication capacity, and thus all of the firms in this group subcontract out the fabrication stage of the manufacturing process to other semiconductor firms. While most of the technology-licensing agreements are part of broader alliances with wafer fabrication foundries, design houses also license technology to other semiconductor manufacturers and receive royalties on sales by these latter firms. Higher levels of cooperation are less common among the design houses: of the twenty-four in the sample, seven (29%) maintain one or more cooperative technology-development agreements with other semiconductor firms; none of the design houses are involved in manufacturing joint ventures. The heavy emphasis on technology licensing, and the paucity of more intensive cooperative agreements, suggests that for most design houses, at least, the shift to an extended-network organizational model has not yet occurred. Rather, linkages with other semiconductor firms are driven by short-term constraints imposed by the high capital costs involved in building a new wafer fabrication facility.

The number of agreements is greater on average among semiconductor firms with in-house fabrication capacity. Wafer fabrication firms maintain an average of 5.1 high-interaction agreements, of which the majority are technology-licensing agreements (2.3) and cooperative technology-development agreements (1.7). Of the forty-eight wafer fabrication firms, seventeen (35.4%) do all of their semiconductor production in-house and do not maintain any production agreements with outside foundries. The remaining thirty-one firms (64.6%) subcontract out at least a part of their wafer fabrication to outside firms. The sampled firms maintain an average of 0.9 foundry agreements. The majority of the sampled firms (79.2%) maintain technology-licensing agreements with outside firms, and a large proportion (68.8%) are also involved in cooperative technology-development agreements. In short, these data indicate a considerable degree of interlinkage and cooperation involving the sampled semiconductor firms.

There is, however, considerable variation among the sampled fabrication firms in their degree of involvement in the four types of agreements. Of the forty-eight fabrication firms, seven (14.6%) are involved in ten or more agreements with other semiconductor manufacturers, including numerous wide-ranging cooperative technology-development agreements and manufacturing joint ventures. These firms are generally leading-edge, large- and mid-size producers operating in a variety of product markets using costly submicron process technologies. A second group of firms has a smaller number of licensing and cooperative agreements that are typically focused on one or two key alliances. Of the forty-eight fabrication firms, ten (20.8%) report no currently active licensing or cooperative technology-development agreements. These firms maintain a more traditional stand-alone organizational structure with no substantial cooperative linkage with other semiconductor firms. The data suggest that, with the exception of a small number of medium-size and large firms, the level of interconnection among firms remains somewhat constrained. Nevertheless, it is precisely those medium-size and large producers who maintain an extensive web of interconnections that represent the most technologically advanced firms within the industry.

Some sense of the diversity of agreements can be gained by considering the alliances established by three U.S. firms during the 1980s. Figure 5.2 shows the major agreements for VLSI Technology, Advanced Micro Devices (AMD), and Xilinx. The pattern of agreements for VLSI Technology and AMD is typical for mid-size U.S. semiconductor manufacturers. Both firms have major technology and production partnerships with other semiconductor manufacturers, as well as a number of ancillary technological agreements. VLSI Technology currently has major agreements with three Japanese firms (Hitachi, Sanyo, and Nippon Steel) and one U.S. firm (Intel). Advanced Micro Devices maintains major partnerships with Fujitsu (for Erasable Programmable Read Only Memory (EPROM) and flash memory) and Sony (for Very Large Scale Integration (VLSI) technology). Xilinx, a small start-up semiconductor firm, has a more limited set of interfirm alliances, the primary one being a foundry agreement with Seiko. While there are some similarities in the pattern of alliances of each firm, the specific alliances reflect differences in the manufacturing competencies and competitive positions of the three firms.

Advanced Micro Devices, established in 1969 as a manufacturer of commodity integrated circuits, is the oldest of the

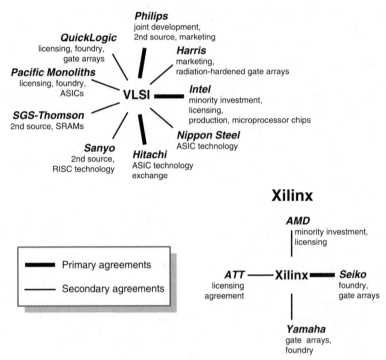

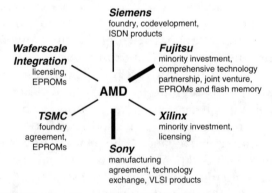

FIGURE 5.2. Strategic agreements of three semiconductor firms.

three firms.[2] It is currently the fifth largest merchant semiconductor manufacturer in the United States, producing a broad range of commodity and ASSP products. With extensive in-house manufacturing capability and a series of successful proprietary product lines, the agreement structure of AMD is typical of that for many large semiconductor manufacturers. Through the mid-1980s, AMD's alliances with other semiconductor firms were limited to second-source agreements (including overflow subcontracting arrangements) and product-specific technology-licensing agreements, the most significant of which was the licensing of the microcode for the 8086 microprocessor from Intel Corporation. Throughout the 1980s, AMD was one of the strongest proponents of the U.S. model of entrepreneurial industrialization and of the need to maintain an independent semiconductor industry in the United States. The president of the company, W. J. Sanders, has been highly critical of government orchestrated collaboration (Sematech) and of the proliferation of technology alliances between U.S. and Japanese firms. Nevertheless, in the late 1980s AMD signed a major production and technology agreement with Sony. In 1992 AMD signed a second partnership agreement, this time with Fujitsu.

What was the rationale for these agreements? Why has AMD moved away from its exclusive commitment to in-house production and technology development? The agreement with Sony was primarily motivated by a desire to improve manufacturing performance. During the mid-1980s, AMD came under increasing pressure in key commodity product markets, losing market share to Japanese firms that were achieving higher yields on the production line. The Sony agreement is a mechanism for AMD to learn Japanese manufacturing practices. Under the terms of the agreement, Sony purchased AMD's San Antonio fabrication facility and gained access to certain AMD proprietary technologies. In addition, however, Sony agreed to serve as a foundry for AMD products, and to transfer manufacturing expertise to AMD. AMD's engineers

[2]The company began business as a second-source supplier and subsequently developed a series of proprietary product technologies.

work alongside Sony's engineers in the San Antonio facility. The choice of Sony, rather than of any other Japanese firm, reflects in part the fact that Sony's major product lines do not directly compete with those of AMD.

AMD's second major agreement, signed with Fujitsu, is more extensive and farreaching than the alliance with Sony. The Fujitsu alliance involves a commitment to construct a jointly owned production facility in Japan, and to jointly develop products, such as EPROM and flash memory devices. In this case, the alliance is driven, above all, by the rising manufacturing costs of submicron based integrated circuits. As development and production costs rose during the 1980s, it became difficult for even large firms to sustain the levels of R&D and capital investment necessary to remain on the leading-edge of technology development. The problem has become especially acute in highly competitive commodity product markets, where market share and return on investment are highly uncertain. The AMD-Fujitsu alliance is an agreement to share the costs and risks of new technology-development and production. In addition to its R&D costs of approximately $50 million per annum, the new manufacturing plant has an estimated cost of $700 million. Problems of competition are dealt with in the alliance in two ways. First, the jointly owned factory will be the only source of advanced flash memory for the two firms. Second, the firms have agreed to divide geographical markets among themselves so as not to compete against each other for the same customers (i.e., preexisting design-in agreements with customers constitute one of the important complementary assets that help to avoid turning the cooperative relationship into a competitive one).

The rising cost of leading-edge process technology and production facilities also underlies the alliances maintained by VLSI Technology and Xilinx. Both firms have signed manufacturing agreements with Japanese producers. In 1988, VLSI Technology entered into an agreement with Hitachi that provided access to the Japanese company's 1.0 and 0.8 micron process technology and to its manufacturing facilities as back-up foundry capacity (Hitachi gained access to VLSI's ASIC design technology). The agreement was extended in 1992 to include Hitachi's leading-edge 0.6 and 0.45 micron processes.

VLSI Technology also has second-source agreements with SGS-Thompson (for static random access memories [SRAMs]), Sanyo (for reduced instruction set computing [RISC] micro-processors), and Intel (for PC chipsets). Xilinx is a start-up manufacturer of field-programmable gate arrays that sub-contracts out all of its device-fabrication needs to other semi-conductor firms, including Seiko and Yamaha in Japan. These agreements of VLSI Technology and Xilinx are the subject of considerable controversy in the semiconductor industry. In return for guaranteed access to leading-edge production capac-ity, VLSI Technology and Xilinx (as well as many other start-up semiconductor firms) have transferred key product designs and design-software systems to their Japanese suppliers.

VLSI Technology and Xilinx maintain several other alliances that are illustrative of the range of interests served by interfirm agreements (see Figure 5.2). In the late 1980s, VLSI signed an agreement with the Dutch electronics firm Philips. VLSI's interest in this partnership derives from the extensive marketing infrastructure maintained by the Dutch firm in Eu-rope. Close contact with customers is especially important in the manufacture of the ASIC and ASSP products that domi-nate much of VLSI's product lines. The partnership with Phil-ips allows VLSI to expand its sales in the European market. VLSI Technology's licensing agreements with QuickLogic and Pacific Monoliths, by contrast, are intended to broaden the range of ASIC product designs that VLSI is able to man-ufacture, facilitating "one-stop-shopping" by major customers. By licensing the product technologies of other firms, VLSI is able to make full use of its manufacturing capacity and strategic partnerships with major customers.

Of the various marketing, research, production, and tech-nology agreements to be observed in the industry, two types are of particular significance: (a) foundry agreements; and (b) sub-micron technology development agreements. These will now be examined in greater detail.

Foundry Agreements

The questionnaire survey obtained information on the amount of wafer fabrication performed in-house and by external subcontractors. Table 5.2 presents the findings for seventy-two firms surveyed in 1990. Data are provided for all firms, and separately for design houses and for firms possessing in-house fabrication facilities. In calculating group means, the percentages provided by each of the sampled firms are weighted by that firm's total sales of integrated circuits. In addition, note that manufacturing facilities owned jointly with another firm (i.e. manufacturing joint ventures) are counted as in-house production capability.

By definition, design houses do not have in-house wafer fabrication capability; all of their production is done by external subcontractors. The twenty-four design houses in the survey sample had 20.0% of their wafer fabrication (by value) performed by other U.S. firms, and the remaining 80.0% by foreign semiconductor manufacturers. For the firms that operate their own wafer fabrication facilities, a weighted average of 88.5% of their fabrication work was performed in-house, 2.9% was done by other U.S. firms, and 8.6% by foreign firms. Of the total amount of wafer fabrication performed by external subcontractors, 23.7% was carried out by U.S. firms and 76.3% by foreign firms, confirming the dominant role of Japanese and other Asian manufacturers as wafer fabrication foundries.

U.S. semiconductor firms, whether large or small, subcontract out some percentage of their wafer fabrication needs. Firms possessing in-house fabrication capacity use outside foundries primarily as overflow subcontractors when demand outstrips available in-house capacity. This form of subcontract-

TABLE 5.2. Percentage of Wafer Fabrication Performed In-House and by External Subcontractors, by Value, 1990[a]

		Subcontractors	
	In-house	U.S. firms	Foreign firms
Design houses	0.0	20.0	80.0
Fabrication firms	88.5	2.9	8.6
All firms	84.4	3.7	11.9

[a]In calculating the group means, percentages for each sampled firm are weighted by total integrated-circuit sales.

ing is common throughout many industries and is typically known as volume subcontracting (Holmes 1986). In the case of design houses, outside subcontractors are used as the exclusive source of wafer fabrication capacity. In general, the emergence of these vertically disintegrated design houses reflects the rising costs of wafer fabrication facilities. With the cost of even low-volume fabrication facilities (so-called mini-fabs) exceeding $80 million, small firms have had great difficulty raising sufficient venture capital to provide in-house fabrication capability. Accordingly, the majority of start-up firms have turned to outside foundries for wafer fabrication. As indicated in Table 5.2, 80.0% of the foundry work for the sampled design houses is performed by foreign firms, primarily Japanese and South Korean semiconductor manufacturers.

NO

Partnership agreements between U.S. design houses and foreign wafer fabrication foundries represent a substantial proportion of the total number of strategic alliances established during the 1980s. They are also the most hotly contested of the various types of agreements observed in the semiconductor industry. Supporters of foundry agreements suggest that the use of external foundries is a positive development; such agreements match the design expertise of one firm with the production capability of another in ways that allow the realization of economies of scale in production (through the pooling of the production requirements of several firms) and the vigorous pursuit of new product technologies by many small firms. Critics charge that this production form is not sustainable over the long term; in their view, externalization of wafer fabrication undermines important synergies between product and process technology and facilitates an accelerated diffusion of technology to competing firms. The issues of synergy and technology diffusion are addressed in turn below.

One of the major criticisms of foundry relationships is that coordination of product and process technologies is more effective when wafer fabrication is performed in-house. By this account, the use of external foundries undermines the flow of information between product and process engineers, and generates difficulties in solving yield and performance problems on the production line. In practice, however, much of the wafer fabrication work performed by outside foundries is based on relatively mature process technologies. Because these technologies are well characterized, and because their performance is well understood, yield problems and device failure are less likely to occur. Under these circumstances, the foundry relationship is more routinized than is the case with leading-edge process technologies, and more easily managed as an external subcontract arrangement.

Just what constitutes a mature or leading-edge semiconductor process technology is an issue of some complexity. One rough indicator, however, is the level of miniaturization of the process, and in particular, whether the technology involves submicron production. In general, the shift to submicron production has occurred earlier among vertically integrated firms that operate their own fabrication facilities. Of the twenty-four design houses participating in the questionnaire survey, more than half (thirteen firms) reported that they were not yet manufacturing products using submicron process technology. In short, many design houses are "design" rather than "process" driven, basing their competitive advantage on the quality of the circuit design rather than on the use of the very latest process technology. Under these conditions, the use of outside foundries is a competitive organizational solution. Where competitive advantage depends on the use of leading-edge process technology, the tendency is toward vertical integration of production.

The second major criticism of foundry agreements is that the short-term benefits for design houses are more than outweighed by the long-term costs of transferring technology to outside foundries. The extent of technology transfer stems in large part from the incentives that design houses have to provide to foundries in order to secure guaranteed access to outside fabrication capacity. When the semiconductor industry is in a recession, and overall capacity utilization is low, semiconductor firms are typically able to secure the services of external foundries on a simple subcontract basis. In most cases, however, design houses sign partnership agreements with outside foundries; such agreements guarantee access to production capacity and provide protection against capacity shortfalls during periods of high demand. Typically, these agreements involve the licensing of product technology or design tools to the foundry, along with rights to sell semiconductors based on this technology. Of the twenty-four design houses in the survey sample, eighteen (75%) have signed a technology licensing agreement with one or more of their wafer fabrication partners.

The recent history of the semiconductor industry is replete with examples of wafer fabrication foundries capturing market share on products and design technologies licensed from U.S. start-up firms. The most celebrated examples illustrate the growing dominance of Japanese firms in low-density gate arrays and other ASIC products: initial entry into these markets was based on technology and design software licensed from VLSI Technology, LSI Logic, and other U.S. start-up firms. The crucial question is whether, in signing the licensing agreement, the design house retains exclusive control over some complementary asset in the manufacturing process that can provide the basis for durable competitive advantage. This might involve, for example, licensing a product but not the design tools necessary to develop the next-generation technology. Alternatively, the design house might retain first-mover advantage in the form of cumulative experience and tacit knowledge that is not transferred to the foundry.

In signing technology-licensing agreements, U.S. design houses are clearly becoming more sensitive to these strategic issues. Many of the most recent agreements have been signed with steel manufacturers rather than the major Japanese semiconductor firms in an apparent attempt to maximize first-mover advantage. Paradigm Technology, for example, recently formed a technology partnership with the Japanese steel manufacturer NKK. The alliance involves three major agreements. First, Paradigm licenses its current product technology to NKK in return for quarterly cash payments that support new R&D. Second, NKK will provide Paradigm with guaranteed access to volume manufacturing capability at a submicron wafer fabrication facility currently under construction in Japan. Third, the two firms have agreed to joint development of next-generation SRAM technology; products arising from this joint development work will be marketed by NKK in Asia, and by Paradigm in the rest of the world. In short, the alliance is structured to provide Paradigm with some protection against direct competition from NKK primarily through a division of market areas of operation.

These developments notwithstanding, the licensing of technology to foundries is unlikely to be a successful strategy over the long term. Perhaps the major difficulty with this strategy is that the flow of knowledge and experience tends to be unidirectional, from the design house to the foundry; because little of the foundry's production expertise flows back to the design house, only the foundry can realize synergies in both the product design and the production stages of the manufacturing process. In addition, the recent tendency to specify market areas of operation as a defense against direct competition will likely be undermined by the increasing globalization of semiconductor manufacturing operations. At the present time, both U.S. and Japanese semiconductor firms have strong design-in linkages with their national markets that reinforce contractual agreements to divide markets on a geographical basis. Japanese semiconductor firms, for example, have long-standing ties with Japanese customers that make it difficult for U.S. firms to capture a share of the market in Japan. As customer–supplier linkage becomes globalized, and the allegiance to domestic suppliers weakens, U.S. semiconductor firms will experience increased sales opportunities in Japan. The lure of increased sales will tend to undermine market share agreements among U.S. and Japanese semiconductor firms.

Submicron Process Agreements

The second major category of manufacturing partnerships involves the codevelopment of process technology and production capability. As we have seen, the primary motivation for the formation of these partnerships is the rapid increase in R&D, equipment, and facility costs associated with the shift to submicron wafer fabrication.

Table 5.3 shows a sample of recent process-technology development agreements involving U.S. semiconductor firms.

TABLE 5.3. Selected Submicron Process-Technology Development Agreements

Partner firms	Date initiated	Technology focus
Altera–Cypress	1990	CMOS to 0.65 microns
AMD–Sony	1990	CMOS to 0.65 microns
AMD–Fujitsu	1992	Flash memory
Analog Devices–Hewlett Packard	1992	CMOS and BiCMOS
AT&T–NEC	1990	CMOS to 0.20 microns
IBM–Toshiba	1992	Flash Memory
IBM–Siemens–Toshiba	1992	64M DRAMs
IMP–Seeq	1991	CMOS to 0.65 microns
Intel–Sharp	1992	Flash memory
Motorola–Toshiba	1986	Microprocessors/DRAMs
National Semiconductor–Toshiba	1992	Flash memory
Texas Instruments–Hitachi	1988	64M DRAMs

These agreements take a variety of forms and involve several different types of firms. The majority of the agreements are for the development of process technologies for particular products, such as EPROMs (Altera–Cypress), SRAMs (AMD–Fujitsu and Intel–Sharp), and DRAMs (IBM–Siemens–Toshiba and Texas Instruments–Hitachi). Other agreements, such as the one between AT&T and NEC, are more far-reaching, involving cooperation across a wide range of research areas. While some agreements extend to joint production (e.g., Motorola–Toshiba and AMD–Fujitsu), others are limited to R&D only. Most of the participants are large U.S. and Japanese manufacturers.

A recent development has been the involvement of small and mid-size U.S. firms in technology partnerships; the latter firms have formed partnerships both with one another (e.g., Altera–Cypress) and with larger firms (Analog Devices–Hewlett Packard). The effects of rising process-technology costs are especially significant for small and medium-size firms. Analog Devices, for example, had a total R&D budget in 1991 of $90 million, of which approximately $11 million was available for process-technology development. The minimum annual R&D costs for submicron process development are estimated to exceed $25 million.

In short, there are many different types of process-technology agreements. The partnerships that have drawn the greatest interest are those between large leading-edge U.S. and Japanese firms. Brief descriptions of four such partnerships—those between AT&T and NEC; Texas Instruments and Hitachi; Toshiba and Motorola; and IBM, Siemens, and Toshiba—are given below.

The AT&T–NEC alliance, set up in 1990, is a wide-ranging agreement covering more than thirty areas of research, including specific product lines (e.g., SRAMs) as well as complementary metal oxide semiconductor (CMOS) process development to 0.20 microns. The alliance provides for an ongoing exchange of researchers between the firms, and includes a marketing joint venture in Japan (but as yet no joint production).

The Texas Instruments–Hitachi alliance was initially established for the joint development of 16M DRAMs and associated process technology. In 1991 the agreement was extended to the development of next-generation 64M and 256M technology. Although the two firms developed separate design architectures for 16M DRAMs, they intend to develop a common architecture for 64M devices. To this end, the companies have established a joint technology-design center at Texas Instrument's Miho manufacturing facility in Japan. In addition to joint technology development, the two firms cross license technologies and have a mutual supply agreement for DRAMs and other advanced semiconductor products.

The Motorola–Toshiba alliance is the oldest of the four partnerships (National Research Council [1992] has an extended discussion of this alliance). Established in 1986, the alliance provides for the transfer of Motorola's microprocessor technology in return for Toshiba's expertise in DRAM manufacturing, and for the use of Toshiba's customer contacts to increase Motorola's share of the Japanese market. Motorola and Toshiba manufacture DRAMs and microprocessors at a jointly owned manufacturing facility in Japan (Tohoku Semiconductor).

Toshiba is also involved in a major alliance with IBM and Siemens for the development of 64M DRAMs. To date, this three-way partnership remains a research endeavor only, with product design taking place at IBM's advanced technology division facilities in East Fishkill, New York, and Burlington, Vermont.

The pairing of major producers in the United States and Japan constitutes a major shift in the terms of competition and cooperation in the semiconductor industry. Two issues are of particular note in this regard. First, the "partnerships of the strong" are characterized by a more balanced flow of knowledge and technology, as compared to the largely one-way flow of technology that characterized the earlier alliances between U.S. start-up firms and large Japanese manufacturers. While some difficulties have been encountered (e.g., by Motorola in transferring knowledge and technology from the Tohoku joint venture to other manufacturing plants), several of the alliances have already been renewed for the development of next-generation technology.[3] In many cases, the expertise of U.S. firms in product technology is matched with Japanese prowess in process technology and high-volume production. The focus of these partnerships, however, is not so much on the transfer of existing technology as on the sharing of the cost of developing next-generation products and production processes.

Second, and as a corollary to the first issue, the emergence of successful global alliances has the potential to shift competition away from the current, predominantly nationalistic focus to a struggle among competing global partnerships. Indeed, several analysts have suggested that the emerging partnership agreements between major U.S. and Japanese firms will likely form the basis for a series of global semiconductor "camps," each centered on the process-technology capabilities of two or three global firms linked to a multitude of smaller, allied producers. Henceforth, it is argued, the primary axis of competi-

---

[3]It is interesting, in this regard, that we know relatively little about the barriers to effective international cooperation in technology-intensive industries. With the policy focus centered on the direction of the technology flow, little attention has been paid to the conditions under which international cooperation can be effectively sustained. Research by Westney (1991), among others, suggests that differences in managerial culture, norms, and expectations (e.g., over appropriate rates of return on basic research) are likely to be significant obstacles to successful cooperation between U.S. and Japanese semiconductor firms.

tion will not be between the United States and Japan, but between competing camps of global producers.

It is worth noting in this regard that most U.S. semiconductor manufacturers have chosen to partner with a foreign rather than a domestic firm: AT&T with NEC, Hitachi with Toshiba, and so on. Critics have charged that this international linkage simply reflects a desire on the part of Japanese firms for access to U.S. technology (Prestowitz 1988). Interviews with U.S. semiconductor manufacturers suggest a different interpretation, namely, that foreign partnerships are *more* likely to provide complementary expertise, and are *less* likely to result in direct competition between partner firms. This argument is consistent with the conceptual framework laid out earlier in the chapter. Because most of the large U.S. semiconductor manufacturers are in direct competition with one another across a wide range of markets, it would be difficult for these firms to identify the complementary assets outside of the partnership necessary to prevent a collaboration from collapsing into competition. When U.S. firms form partnerships with Japanese producers, by contrast, collaboration is supported by the advantage each firm retains in selling products within its domestic market; each can draw on existing customer relations that are hard for foreign producers to replicate in the short term. In addition, U.S. and Japanese firms often emphasize different product technologies, and these differences are an additional defense against abrogation of the partnership agreement.

At the present time, the allegiance of most U.S. semiconductor firms to any particular international partner is weak. The durability of existing partnerships is uncertain, dependent on the ability of the firms to generate new technologies from the cooperative venture and to avoid direct competition with one another. The situation, moreover, is often complex: two firms that cooperate in one technology market (e.g., SRAMs) may be competitors in another (e.g., ASICs). At the same time, Japanese semiconductor firms typically maintain partnerships with several U.S. manufacturers who are in direct competition with one another. For example, in addition to its partnerships with Motorola and IBM, Toshiba also maintains an agreement with National Semiconductor for fast-logic and flash-memory devices, and has recently announced an additional technology-development agreement with Samsung.[4] While working with Texas Instruments on DRAM technology, Hitachi also collaborates with Hewlett Packard (on RISC microprocessors) and VLSI Technology (on ASIC products).

Of central concern to U.S. policymakers is the likely impact of emergent technology partnerships on employment. This issue may be addressed, first, in terms of the primary location of the collaborative activity. To date, with the exception of a small number of production joint ventures, the majority of technology partnerships have not involved the construction of new research or manufacturing facilities. Collaboration takes place through the exchange of researchers and engineers among the partner firms, and through the use of existing facilities. With respect to R&D, the location of collaborative activity is fairly evenly balanced between the United States and Japan. In the case of 64M DRAMs, for example, the IBM–Toshiba–Siemens project is based in the United States, and the Texas Instruments–Hitachi project is centered in Japan. Production joint ventures, however, have a rather different geography: virtually all of the production facilities are located in Japan (including the joint ventures operated by LSI Logic and Kawasaki Steel, Motorola and Toshiba, Texas Instruments and Kobe Steel, and the recently announced partnership between AMD and Fujitsu.) In most cases, the selection of Japanese sites for joint ventures is driven by the desire to draw on the production expertise of the Japanese partner. The concentration of production joint ventures in Japan raises the specter of a progressive loss of manufacturing employment in the United States. As the number of manufacturing joint ventures increases, however, and as the manufacturing performance of U.S. firms continues to improve, it is likely that the location of

---

[4]Unlike DRAMs, flash-memory devices retain information even after the power supply is turned off. Most analysts predict a huge market for the devices, which are being promoted as an alternative form of data storage to hard-disk drives in computers. While flash-memory technology was initially developed by Toshiba in the mid-1980s, Intel currently dominates the market. The technology-development agreement between Toshiba and Samsung illustrates well the complexity of alliances: the two firms will now cooperate in flash memory and compete in DRAMs.

such joint ventures will extend beyond Japan to the United States. As with the wholly owned branch plants of Japanese firms currently located in the United States, proximity to major market areas is also likely to motivate the location of production joint ventures in the United States. Encouraging this development should be a central policy objective of the U.S. government

Because international alliances are a relatively new phenomenon in the semiconductor industry, it is difficult to assess their long-term implications for employment. Little information is available, for example, on the pattern of customer and supplier linkages associated with international joint ventures. Moreover, it remains far from clear how the results of collaborative technology-development will be incorporated into the internal manufacturing operations of partner firms. Additional research is needed in order to assess the economic effects of international alliances on specific geographic regions.

CONCLUSION

For much of the past decade, international partnerships have been viewed as a source of competitive disadvantage for U.S. semiconductor firms (Reich and Mankin 1986). In retrospect, it is clear that many alliances were poorly structured, both in terms of the direction of the flow of technology, and in terms of the extent to which U.S. firms retained control over the complementary assets necessary to secure competitive advantage in semiconductor manufacturing. Many partnerships involved a trade-off between short-term gain (e.g., access to additional production capacity or investment credit) and mid- to long-term disadvantage (the accelerated transfer of technology to foreign competitors). Of particular concern in this regard have been the partnerships formed between U.S. start-up firms and Japanese semiconductor foundries (National Academy of Sciences 1992). Acting from a position of weakness, with only limited venture capital available for production facilities, U.S. start-up firms entered into technology-licensing agreements that provided for the transfer of key product and process technologies to offshore foundries.

The motivation for forming interfirm partnerships has increased in recent years, driven by the rising cost of process technology and leading-edge production facilities, the emergence of new markets for low-volume, design-intensive devices, and the globalization of demand for semiconductor products. In the face of these developments, U.S. firms have sought to share the risk and cost of semiconductor manufacturing through the formation of various types of manufacturing partnerships and strategic alliances. These partnerships are now emerging as a crucial aspect of the competitive strategies of U.S. semiconductor firms. In establishing the most recent partnerships, U.S. firms, apparently having learnd from the mistakes of the past, have been careful to ensure that cooperation with partners does not erode competitive advantage. In the case of technology-development agreements, knowledge and information generated by the partnership are generally combined with the specialized market and product technology of each partner firm, thereby discouraging direct competition among the partners. U.S. semiconductor firms are also exploring other ways of financing new capital and R&D investments, such as enticing customers to invest in the firms' fabrication facilities.

Although the proliferation of technology alliances in the semiconductor industry has been in response to the specific technological and market conditions of the industry, there is now a growing body of literature suggesting that such manufacturing partnerships are becoming increasingly common in other technologically dynamic sectors of production (Contractor and Lorange 1988; Link and Bauer 1989; Mowery 1988; Mytelka 1990). But is the spreading of alliances a transitional phenomenon, one destined to be followed by new rounds of concentration and centralization within integrated global corporations? The answer to this question hinges on the relative efficiency of different organizational forms. In this regard, partnerships and alliances are appropriately seen as one expression of a more general form of 'network' organization that lies between pure market transactions and the internal activities of individual firms (Camagni 1991; Hakansson 1987; Storper 1992). Long-term trust based relations among a network of producers reduce the governance costs typically associated with pure market transactions, while avoiding the up front costs of providing all manufacturing needs in-house. Partnerships and alliances create a set of organized relations among specialized producers and provide individual firms access to a wide variety of manufacturing capabilities.

Storper (1992, p. 79) suggests that the advantage of production networks over both the individual firm and the pure market is that networks allow firms greater flexibility in redeploying manufacturing resources into different products and production processes, thus reducing the likelihood of "lock-in" to suboptimal technological trajectories while also reducing overall production cost.

Avoidance of lock-in is of particular importance in technologically dynamic industries, where the path of technological development remains uncertain and is often subject to change (Foray 1993). As manufacturing systems are recentered on a dynamic of continuous innovation and rapid technological change, the importance of such manufacturing flexibility is likely to increase. In the case of the semiconductor industry, interfirm partnerships do not just provide manufacturers with the flexibility to shift among different technological pathways; they are, more immediately, a mechanism for sharing investment risk in a highly uncertain and rapidly changing technological environment. Rather than betting the firm on the success of new product and process technologies, semiconductor manufacturers are able to share costs and risks with other producers operating in complementary product markets.

Although strategic alliances have emerged as an important organizational feature of the semiconductor industry, it is important to emphasize that they are not a cure for the competitive problems of U.S. firms. Strategic alliances between U.S. and Japanese firms are neither the primary cause of the recent loss of market share by U.S. firms, nor the most important explanation for the current stabilization of the U.S. semiconductor industry. As indicated in the previous chapter, the rebuilding of the U.S. semiconductor industry depends, above all, on continued improvements in production performance

and in time-to-market for new products and production processes. Nevertheless, the proliferation of international alliances
has changed the terms of competition in the semiconductor
industry, and has called into question the role of the U.S.
government in promoting the U.S. semiconductor industry.
With the increasing globalization of semiconductor manufacturing, the presumed linkage between the welfare of U.S.-
based firms and the welfare of the U.S. economy is weakened. I
now turn to the role of government policy, and more generally
to the ways in which the performance of U.S. semiconductor
firms is shaped by various forms of direct and indirect government intervention in the industry.

CHAPTER 6

Government Intervention in the Semiconductor Industry

T his chapter assesses the contribution of government intervention to the changing fortunes of the U.S. semiconductor industry during the 1980s. Throughout the decade, the industry was at the forefront of a wide-ranging policy debate concerning the appropriate role for government agencies in supporting the growth of U.S. firms and industries. Much of the debate was focused on whether it is desirable for governments to provide targeted aid to selected industries experiencing competitive difficulties. More generally, a series of questions have been raised concerning the efficacy of industrial intervention by national governments in an era of intensified globalization of markets, trade, and production. U.S. trade and technology policy is apparently at a turning point, with the semiconductor industry being the primary arena within which the policy debate is to be played out.

The policies and programs of federal, state, and local governments have always had a major impact on the fortunes of U.S. high-technology industries. The vision of a free market, in which the hand of government is absent, is a myth that has now been laid to rest. In the case of the semiconductor industry, for example, U.S. firms have received substantial benefit from defense and space initiatives, both in the form of direct support for R&D and, more importantly, in the form of military procurement programs. Indeed, the economic effects of various defense buildups have been so great that Markusen et al. (1991)

describe military programs as a hidden industrial policy that has contributed to the rise of Southern California and other parts of the U.S. "Gunbelt" in the second half of the twentieth century.

Whatever the actual economic impact of military procurement may be the *asserted* rationale for this and other government programs is their contribution to a public interest (in this case national defense) rather than to the economic prosperity of private firms and individual industries. During the 1980s, the dominant political-economic philosophy within the U.S. government was one of opposition to industrial policy: the market was believed to provide the best mechanism for allocating resources among firms and industries, and among national and regional economies. Government intervention was seen as an option of last resort, to be supported only under conditions of demonstrated market failure. While the decline of individual industries was an issue of concern, the role of government was to facilitate and ease the social costs of economic adjustment through worker retraining schemes, unemployment compensation, and other allied programs.

During the past decade a contrasting theoretical position gained support. It suggests that free markets and minimal government involvement in advanced industrial economies do not always generate the highest industrial growth-rates or the greatest social welfare (Krugman 1986; Tyson 1992). Where industrial production is characterized by dynamic economies of scale, imperfect competition, and a cumulative and territorially embedded knowledge base, government intervention can decisively shift competitive advantage from one national economy to another. For many, the rise of Japan to a position of market leadership in high-technology industries is a paradigmatic example of the positive growth-effects of aggressive government intervention (Prestowitz 1988). Through a combination of investment incentives, coordination of R&D, and market closure, the Japanese government helped to secure the rise of the Japanese semiconductor industry to a position of market leadership, thereby undermining the profitability of, and employment in, the U.S semiconductor industry. By this account, the United States should learn from the Japanese experience and implement a national technology and trade initiative of its own, one designed to ensure the competitiveness of U.S. firms in global markets. Other researchers, however, have been more pessimistic about the feasibility or desirability of increased government intervention in high-technology industries (e.g., Flamm 1991).

Much of the debate has been waged around the issue of government support for the semiconductor industry. Opposition to industrial policy notwithstanding, the U.S. government initiated during the 1980s two major new programs of support for the U.S. semiconductor industry: a semiconductor trade agreement with Japan, and multiyear financing for a consortium of U.S. semiconductor firms (Sematech). The attention paid to the semiconductor industry derives in part from a widely held belief that the competitive difficulties of U.S. semiconductor firms are directly traceable to unfair competition from Japan. In addition, the U.S. semiconductor industry has conducted a highly effective lobbying campaign, led by the Semiconductor Industry Association (SIA), to convince government officials that the continued prosperity of a domestic semiconductor industry is an issue of national security and thus a legitimate target for government support. In the absence of a strong domestic industry, the SIA argues, U.S. defense interests would be placed at risk by dependence upon foreign sources of supply for leading-edge semiconductor devices. Whatever the validity of this argument, the implementation of the U.S.–Japan trade agreement, and the funding of Sematech, have made the U.S. semiconductor industry something of a test case for industrial policy. To what extent, for example, can the stabilization of the economic fortunes of U.S. firms since the late 1980s be traced to the efforts of Sematech? Has the U.S.–Japan trade agreement had a positive impact on the competitiveness of U.S. semiconductor firms?

TRADE THEORY: THE CASE FOR GOVERNMENT INTERVENTION

Traditional international trade theory is based on the concept of comparative advantage: nations trade to take advantage of differences in existing or constructed resource endowments, specializing in those activities in which they possess comparative advantage. The new trade theory, the origins of which actually go back at least to the 1930s, suggests that to a significant degree nations trade because there are inherent advantages to specialization, advantages that derive from the existence of increasing returns to economic activity (Dixit and Norman 1980; Krugman 1979, 1990a, 1990b). Whether it be Swiss watch makers or German machine-tools manufacturers, as an industry within a country increases in size, various internal and external economies of scale become available, from the emergence of specialized suppliers to the availability of a pool of skilled and experienced workers. To the extent that these increasing returns are captured primarily by domestic firms, growth in an industry can generate advantage over international competitors, leading to a self-reinforcing dynamic of economic specialization among national economies. On the basis of this theory of increasing returns, government policy emerges as a strategic tool that can be used to support the growth of industries to the point where they are able to compete internationally on the basis of self-generated external and internal economies of scale. By providing subsidies, guaranteed markets, trade barriers, and other forms of assistance, governments are in theory able to shift decisively the competitive advantage of a nation's industrial base.

The rapid growth of the semiconductor and other high-technology industries in Japan is often cited as a classic example of the process of strategic government intervention at work. Japanese government support for high-technology firms has taken a number of different forms, including direct subsidy of R&D and protection of the domestic market. Notwithstanding the growing support for government intervention, however, several elements of the analysis remain contentious.

First, it is unclear to what degree external economies generated within an industry are exclusively, or even primarily, available to domestic firms (as opposed to foreign firms). The emergence of specialized semiconductor equipment suppliers in Silicon Valley, for example, will only provide international advantage if U.S. semiconductor firms, because of geography or nationality, have privileged access to the suppliers' knowledge and equipment. And yet one of the key trends of the past two decades has been the increasing globalization of high-technology manufacturing in ways that accelerate the flow of knowledge and information across national boundaries, through international alliances, foreign investment, and off-shore production. Nelson and Wright (1992), among others, have suggested that such globalization of manufacturing systems undermines the value of strategic government intervention in support of high-technology industries, (what these authors label "techno-economic nationalism").

In many ways the point of contention is now less whether high-technology industries are characterized by external economies of scale than to what degree the latter economies are captured by domestic firms. The degree of capture depends in large part upon the openness of the technology environment (see Chapter 3); industry observers charge that U.S. firms do not have the same access to Japanese technology that Japanese firms have to U.S. technology. In making the case for Sematech, for example, it is often claimed that Japanese equipment suppliers allow privileged access to Japanese semiconductor firms, giving the latter competitive advantage in the development of next generation process technologies (National Advisory Committee on Semiconductors [NACS] 1989). Close ties between equipment suppliers and device manufacturers in Japan, often supported by cross-investment and other Keiretsu linkages, provided Japanese firms with early access to leading-edge equipment technologies. What distinguishes the Japanese case is less the existence of government support for high technology firms than the degree to which that support benefits primarily domestic producers. By this account, the policy debate should focus not on the presence or absence of R&D subsidies and allied forms of government support, but on the issue of equal international access to the technologies and suppliers receiving the support (see also Ostry 1990).

On a related theme, Reich (1991) has called into question the intended target of government intervention. Is government support to be directed toward U.S.-owned firms, or toward all firms (domestic or foreign) operating within the United States? In the face of increasing internationalization of production, it is far from clear whether support for U.S.-owned firms will translate into the greatest number of high-income jobs for U.S. workers. By the same token, the growing amount of foreign investment in the United States suggests that the U.S.-based operations of foreign firms would be legitimate beneficiaries of government support. At issue here is the precise way in which the internationalization of economic processes is taking place within high-technology industries and other sectors of production. If the global corporation is becoming a reality in the sense that its allegiance to any national economy is eroding, then, as Reich (1991) suggests, government support should be available to all firms (both domestic and foreign) operating within the United States.

One additional line of critique focuses on the efficacy of government as an agent of industrial and technological development. Notwithstanding the desirability of providing strategic support for an industry, many researchers question the ability of government to achieve the desired goal (Flamm 1991). While intervention may have facilitated a process of technological catch-up in Japan, governments have a relatively poor record in charting the technological pathways of the future. Critics of increased government intervention point to the less than successful experience of the European Community (EC): high tariff barriers and a multibillion dollar government sponsored research effort (known as JESSI) have done little to alter the competitive prospects of European semiconductor firms. More generally, to the extent that policies of support are adopted by several governments, the possibility exists for very costly duplication of effort as governments compete in an escalating drive to outspend each other in industrial support.

GOVERNMENT INTERVENTION: THE U.S. CASE

While most of the policy debate has focused on government-sponsored R&D, the competitiveness of U.S. semiconductor firms is influenced by a wide variety of government programs and initiatives, and by the regulatory and fiscal environment of the national economy as a whole. Table 6.1 provides an over-

TABLE 6.1. Selected Government Actions Impacting on Semiconductor Firms

Primary rationale for intervention	Actions
Market failure	R&D tax credits
	Worker retraining initiatives
	Equipment depreciation allowance
	Patent protection
	Semiconductor Chip Protection Act (1984)
	Standard setting
	Semiconductor Research Corporation
Collusive behavior	Sherman Antitrust Act
	Semiconductor Trade Agreement (1986, 1991)
	National Cooperative Research Act (1984)
	Exon–Florio amendment
	Section 301 provisions of Trade Act (1988)
	Structural Impediments Initiative (1989)
National interests	Defense and space procurement
	Defense R&D (DARPA, Air Force, etc.)
	Department of Energy R&D (Sandia National Laboratory)
	National Science Foundation: basic R&D
	Sematech

view of U.S. government programs that impact directly on the semiconductor industry. The policy initiatives cover a wide range of activities, from R&D tax credits to intellectual property rights and government procurement. Three broad groups of initiatives can be identified, based on the underlying rationale for intervention. These groups are listed for illustrative purposes only; specific policy initiatives are typically based on a variety of complementary and sometimes cross-cutting interests. For example, while research conducted for the Department of Defense derives in the first instance from national security concerns, this activity also helps to alleviate a widely perceived problem of underfunding of high-technology R&D within the domestic economy.

The programs in the first group are in response to conditions of market failure. It is now well-established that, in the absence of government intervention, private industry tends to under-invest relative to socially desirable norms in the development of public goods and in activities from which firms are unable to appropriate sufficient proprietary benefit. In the case of the semiconductor and other high-technology industries, one of the primary problems is that of underinvestment in R&D. There is now a large body of research documenting the problems of appropriability associated with R&D, and more generally, the tendency for R&D to generate social returns that are greater than the returns appropriated by private firms (Arrow 1962; Cohen and Levin 1989; Nelson 1959). Underinvestment in R&D is a serious problem in U.S. high-technology industries, a fact that was recently underscored by a series of reports indicating that the rate of investment in R&D by U.S. firms is less than that of firms in Japan, the former West Germany, and other international rivals (National Science Board 1991). Under conditions of market failure, governments can secure higher levels of investment directly, for example, by sponsoring additional R&D. The U.S. government currently sponsors much of the basic R&D underlying the development of semiconductors and other electronics technologies. Governments may also achieve the goal of higher R&D indirectly by changing the costs and benefits associated with investment. Numerous programs help indirectly to secure higher levels of investment in semiconductor R&D, including R&D tax credits, accelerated depreciation allowances, strengthened protection of intellectual property rights, standard setting by government agencies, and military procurement of leading-edge devices (see Table 6.1).

During the early 1980s the U.S. semiconductor industry pushed for stronger patent protection for device technology and secured the passage of the 1984 Semiconductor Chip Protection Act. By strengthening intellectual property rights on semiconductor technology, the government changed the appropriability conditions under which firms are able to secure proprietary benefit from investments, thereby increasing the incentive to invest in semiconductor technology. As with many aspects of government intervention, however, the full effects of stronger intellectual property protection on innovation and technology development are far from clear. Although stronger patent protection increases the returns to innovators and should therefore draw additional investment to the innovation process, it may also slow the adoption of innovations by competing firms and, more generally, undermine the flow of ideas and information among firms. To the extent that the success of U.S. semiconductor firms is based on a dynamic of mutual learning and information exchange, a regulatory environment of aggressive patent protection and attendant litigation may actually undermine a key element of the technology-development process. In addition, venture capitalists would likely respond to aggressive litigation with a more conservative lending policy, one that delayed the release of venture capital until intellectual property had been clearly established through a new patent.

The experience of the Semiconductor Chip Protection Act is illustrative of many of these problems. Two points are of particular importance in this regard (see Rauch 1993). First, rather than amending general copyright law, the 1984 Chip Protection Act created independent property-right protection for semiconductor circuit designs (or more specifically, for the individual layers that collectively constitute the architecture of a semiconductor chip). However, so-called reverse engineering—a practice whereby firms disassemble a competitor's semiconductor devices to learn how they work, and use that knowledge in future product development—was specifically excluded from the Act. Unlike the simple copying of competitors' devices, reverse engineering was seen by U.S. semiconductor firms as a legitimate business practice, one that is necessary for the dynamic of innovation in semiconductors to proceed. Second, a number of technological developments in semiconductors have undermined the commercial opportunities associated with the kinds of direct copying of circuits that the Act was designed to prevent. Even with a photographic copy of circuit architecture in hand, the ability to produce semiconductors is dependent on having access to matched process technology and compatible software tools. With the movement away from commodity circuits, and the increasing specialization of process technologies, the opportunities for simply copying a competitor's products have been reduced.[1]

Much of the lobbying effort of semiconductor-industry trade groups is currently focused on obtaining more direct incentives for investment in R&D. For example, the recently released report of the National Advisory Committee on Semiconductors (1992) calls for an extension of the R&D tax credit (and the inclusion of collaborative R&D under the credit guidelines), a shortening of the depreciation schedule on semiconductor manufacturing equipment to three years, and the reinstatement of the investment tax credit on manufacturing equipment.

A second group of government initiatives addresses issues of market competition and, in particular, problems of collusive or monopolistic behavior by semiconductor firms. Of primary concern here are various elements of antitrust and trade legislation. Mowery and Rosenberg (1990) suggest that a strong antitrust policy in the United States has historically protected start-up firms from take-over bids and helped to shape the entrepreneurial pattern of industrialization characteristic of the U.S. semiconductor industry. In the face of a proliferation of foreign takeovers of start-up firms, many now call for a relaxation of antitrust policy to allow greater collaboration among U.S. producers. Of particular interest in this regard has been the 1984 National Cooperative Research Act (NCRA); by excluding "pre-competitive" research from the triple damage provisions of antitrust law, the Act facilitates cooperative research among semiconductor firms. The Semiconductor Industry Association has called for the extension of these indemnity provisions beyond research consortia to production joint ventures.

In addition to antitrust concerns, the profitability of the U.S. semiconductor industry has been strongly influenced by the efforts of the U.S. International Trade Commission (ITC) and the Office of the U.S. Trade Representative to monitor

---

[1]The issue remains of significance in certain high-volume and commodity markets, such as DRAMs and microprocessors. The legal battle between Intel, AMD, and other manufacturers of Intel-clone microprocessor chips is illustrative of continuing battles over intellectual property rights.

and penalize unfair trading practices on the part of foreign competitors selling in U.S. markets. Relevant policy initiatives in this regard include Section 301 and Super 301 provisions of the 1988 Trade Act, as well as President George Bush's Structural Impediments Initiative. Of primary interest, however, is the Semiconductor Trade Agreement signed by Japan and the United States in 1986, and revised in 1991. The primary basis for government intervention in the U.S. semiconductor industry has been the recurrent allegation of unfair competition and collusive behavior on the part of Japanese semiconductor firms. In the face of widespread accusations of dumping of semiconductors in U.S. markets, the U.S. government negotiated floor prices for DRAMs and other memory devices, as well as a promise on the part of Japan to increase purchases of semiconductors from U.S. firms (the effects of this trade initiative on the competitiveness of U.S. firms are discussed in detail later in the chapter).

The third major group of government programs includes those established specifically to serve defense requirements and other national interests. The semiconductor industry is impacted here by various dimensions of defense procurement and military-sponsored R&D. The U.S. government currently spends an estimated $600 million on R&D related to the development of semiconductor devices. Of this amount, approximately $300 million is on R&D conducted for, or on behalf of, the Department of Defense. In addition to expenditures by the Air Force, Army, and Navy, funds are also channelled through the Defense Advanced Research Projects Agency (DARPA), the Strategic Defense Initiative (SDI), and other organizations reporting to the Secretary of Defense. Semiconductor R&D is also conducted under the auspices of the Department of Energy (e.g., at Sandia National Laboratory), the National Bureau of Standards, and the National Science Foundation. Government-sponsored R&D constitutes approximately 15% of the more than $4 billion of semiconductor R&D conducted in the United States (U.S. Congress, Committee on Science, Space, and Technology 1990). Notwithstanding the scale of government R&D expenditures, their commercial benefit to U.S. semiconductor firms *in the short term* has been relatively limited.

The largest amount of government R&D funds has gone to the development of radiation-hardened integrated circuits, which are used almost exclusively for military and space applications, and to the development of gallium arsenide devices (U.S. Congress, Congressional Budget Office 1987). Much of the remainder of defense-related funding has gone into basic research.

The U.S. government in 1987 began a new R&D initiative by providing support to Sematech, a consortium of semiconductor firms involved in the development of advanced semiconductor-manufacturing technology (U.S. Congress, Committee on Science, Space, and Technology 1990; U.S. Congress, Congressional Budget Office 1990). In contrast to earlier R&D programs, such as very high speed integrated circuit (VHSIC) and microwave and millimeter-wave monolithic integrated circuit (MMMIC), which were clearly focused on the product technology requirements of the defense establishment, the primary goal of Sematech has been to restore U.S. competitiveness in semiconductor manufacturing technology. While the case has been made that a strong domestic semiconductor industry serves national defense interests, it is clear that government intervention has been heavily influenced by commercial interests, that is, by a desire to promote growth in the employment and profitability of U.S. semiconductor firms. Behind the veil of defense concerns lies a desire to improve the competitiveness of the domestic semiconductor industry.

While many complain about a general trend toward "over-regulation" of the U.S. economy (e.g., see President's Council on Competitiveness 1992), it is Sematech and the Semiconductor Trade Agreement that have emerged as the focus of contention among policy analysts. For many observers, what is disturbing is less the fact that the U.S. government would provide support to U.S. firms, than the fact that these two initiatives constitute targeted intervention in support of one industry. By this account, the United States would be best served by R&D tax credits, lower interest rates, and other broad-based policies that provide generic support to all industrial sectors; micromanagement of technology development is best left to firms and markets. This position has recently been reaffirmed by Mowery and Rosenberg (1989a, p. 295):

Indeed, given the difficulties that many public programs have encountered in "fine-tuning" the innovation system and commercializing specific technologies, broad policies that are relatively evenhanded in their effects on all sectors may be more attractive and feasible. Since the adoption of new technologies typically places a premium on the skills of the work force, policies to improve the educational preparation of entrants to the work force, to remedy basic skills deficiencies in the employed work force, and to improve job related training of the employed work force may well yield a far greater payoff (albeit in a longer time frame) than a dozen Sematechs.

Sematech and the Semiconductor Trade Agreement provide something of a test case for the contested strategy of targeted intervention. Because both initiatives have been in operation for several years, it is now possible to make a preliminary assessment of the impact of Sematech and the Trade Agreement on the competitiveness of the U.S. semiconductor industry. As indicated earlier, implementation of these two initiatives has coincided with a stabilization of the economic fortunes of U.S. semiconductor firms. Several reports have suggested that targeted government support has played a major role in rebuilding the semiconductor industry (U.S. General Accounting Office [GAO] 1990, 1991). I now examine these claims in detail.

SEMATECH

Sematech (an acronym for semiconductor manufacturing technology) is a nonprofit research consortium of U.S semiconductor producers that was established in 1987 as one response to declining global competitiveness. The original fourteen member companies are shown in Table 6.2. Each of the member firms pays a fee, ranging from $1 million to $15 million, proportional to its annual semiconductor sales. For the past five years, Congress has appropriated annually $100 million in R&D funds for Sematech, with the stipulation that government contributions cannot exceed 50% of the organization's operating budget. Total expenditures by Sematech, including both federal and member contributions, are now in excess of $1

TABLE 6.2. Founding Members of Sematech

Advanced Micro Devices
AT&T
Digital Equipment Corporation
Harris
Hewlett Packard
Intel
IBM
LSI Logic[a]
Micron Technology[a]
Motorola
National Semiconductor
NCR
Rockwell International
Texas Instruments

[a]Withdrew from Sematech in 1992.
Source: Adapted from U.S. General Accounting Office (1992).

billion. In 1987 a parallel organization (Semi/Sematech) was established as a vehicle for representing the interests of semiconductor equipment and materials suppliers in the Sematech consortium.

The original mission of Sematech was to demonstrate the feasibility of manufacturing leading-edge semiconductors using only U.S.-made equipment. With an internal staff as well as engineers seconded from member firms, Sematech was to purchase equipment and establish a leading-edge wafer processing facility. Information gained concerning the performance of manufacturing equipment, and ways of optimizing the construction and operation of the fabrication line, would be transferred back to member firms, in the first instance, and subsequently to the remainder of the U.S. semiconductor industry. Within two years of operation, however, the focus of the consortium had changed dramatically. The major shift comprised a movement away from the on-line testing and optimization of existing manufacturing equipment to the provision of large-scale developmental assistance to U.S. semiconductor equipment manufacturers.

The shift in the focus of Sematech was a response to the rapidly declining competitive position of U.S. equipment and materials suppliers. Quite simply, dependence on the existing infrastructure of U.S. suppliers compromised the goal of establishing a leading-edge process facility. During the 1980s, U.S. equipment suppliers lost their position of technological leadership in lithography, etching, materials purification, and other key areas of semiconductor manufacturing. During the period 1980–89, the share of the worldwide semiconductor equipment market held by U.S. firms declined from 74% to 42%; during these same years, Japanese manufacturers increased their market share from 20% to 48% (Semi/Sematech 1992). Of the top five semiconductor equipment manufacturers in the world, four are Japanese (Tokyo Electron, Nikon, Advantest, and Canon), and only one (Applied Materials) is a U.S.-based firm.

At the core of the declining competitiveness of U.S. equipment manufacturers was a failure to commit sufficient capital to the development of next-generation equipment, a problem that was exacerbated by the small size of most equipment firms and by their notoriously poor relations with semiconductor producers. Only 6% of U.S. equipment and materials suppliers had sales in 1990 of more than $100 million; the majority were small firms with annual sales of less than $25 million. Jointly, these firms were spending at the end of the 1980s approximately $500 million on R&D. U.S. semiconductor producers were spending an additional $300 million on the development of manufacturing equipment technologies (U.S. Congress, Congressional Budget Office 1987). By way of comparison, the total R&D expenditure by U.S. semiconductor firms in 1989 stood at approximately $3 billion, the vast majority of which was devoted to developing product and process technologies. While product development was funded by semiconductor firms, and basic research by various branches of government, an investment gap had emerged in the area of next-generation manufacturing equipment. Several analysts have suggested that the low level of investment in manufacturing equipment (e.g., relative to investments in semiconductor product technology) reflects difficulties experienced by equipment suppliers in appropriating adequate returns on up-front R&D costs. If underinvestment is indeed a case of partial market failure, then some form of collective intervention would be an appropriate response.

During the period 1987–92, Sematech spent $371 million (or 37% of its total budget) on external R&D, primarily in the form of equipment-improvement projects and technology-development contracts with equipment suppliers. Table 6.3 shows equipment-improvement and technology-development contracts issued by Sematech as of mid-1990. The contracts cover a range of technologies. By far the largest amount of funding (a total of $145 million) was devoted to the development of advanced lithography equipment through contracts with Silicon Valley Group (previously the optical lithography division of Perkin Elmer) and GCA. These two firms are illustrative of the changing fortunes of U.S. equipment manufacturers during the 1980s. In 1980 Perkin Elmer and GCA ranked, respectively, first and second in the world in sales of lithography equipment. Over the course of the next decade this leadership position was lost to the Japanese firms Canon and Nikon, both of which received support from the VLSI technology project of the Ministry of International Trade and Industry (MITI). U.S. firms currently hold less than 30% of the worldwide market for semiconductor lithography systems.

Perkin Elmer in 1989 sold the majority holding in its lithography division to Silicon Valley Group. The terms of the sale were complex. IBM became a minority investor in Silicon Valley Group, providing approximately $20 million in R&D funds and agreeing to purchase twenty of the firm's first-generation Micrascan step-and-scan lithography system. In addition, Sematech provided $20 million in R&D funds through a technology-development grant.

Sematech's support for GCA has taken a different form. By the end of the 1980s, GCA had dropped from the list of top lithography manufacturers, partly as a result of delayed product development, but also because of the poor reliability of its equipment. In order to break back into the lithography market, GCA needed to resolve these problems and then convince users that its equipment would stand up under actual manufacturing conditions. With a price tag in excess of $1 million per machine,

TABLE 6.3. Sematech Equipment Contracts as of June 1990

Supplier	Project
Joint Development	
Advanced Production Technology	Wafer cleaning system
AMRAY	Defect imaging
Applied Science and Technology	Plasma etch
ATEQ	Mask exposure
AT&T	Deep ultraviolet resist
Drytek	Plasma etch
Eaton	Metal deposition
Union Carbide/Semi-Gas/Wilson	Gas delivery system
GCA	Optical wafer stepper
Hampshire Instruments	X-ray optics
Hewlett-Packard	Test chips
KLA Instruments	Wafer defects
Lam Research	Chemical vapor deposition
NCR	Isolation process
NIST	Metrology standard
ORASIS	Wafer defect detection
Orchid One	Electron beam microscope
Silicon Valley Group	Lithography system
University of Cincinnati	Plasma etch
Westech Systems	Planarization
Equipment Improvement	
AMRAY	Electron microscope
Anatel/Particle Measuring Systems	Water purity detection
Angstrom Measurements	Electron microscope
Applied Materials	Chemical vapor deposition Cluster tools
Athens	Hydrofluoric reprocessor
GCA	Optical wafer stepper
Genus	Chemical vapor deposition
Insystems	Defect detection
Lam Research	Plasma metal etch
Silicon Valley Group	Vertical furnace

Source: Adapted from U.S. General Accounting Office (1992).

semiconductor firms were unwilling to take the risk of purchasing a GCA wafer stepper. In response to these difficulties, Sematech signed an equipment-improvement contract with GCA. Under the terms of the contract, Sematech purchased fourteen GCA lithography steppers that were installed for testing, optimization, and evaluation at member wafer fabrication facilities. Information gained from "technology in use" is being incorporated by GCA into the development of its next generation of XLS lithography equipment.

Although a full evaluation is some years away, initial evidence suggests that Sematech has had at least partial success in meeting its revised goal of bolstering the capability of domestic equipment suppliers. The impact of Sematech is visible in a number of different areas. First, the decline in worldwide market share of U.S. semiconductor equipment suppliers has essentially been halted. Although detailed statistics are unavailable, the consulting firm VLSI Research estimates that U.S. firms have actually increased their worldwide market share in semiconductor equipment from 42.8% in 1990, to 47.1% in 1991. Several U.S. firms report increased purchases of U.S. equipment as a result of Sematech programs. Almost 80% of the equipment in Motorola's new MOS-11 fabrication facility, for example, will be manufactured in the United States. Intel announced the purchase of an additional $150 million of equipment and materials from U.S. firms, purchases that were originally scheduled for foreign suppliers (U.S. GAO 1992). Second, according to a General Accounting Office (1992) report, Sematech is widely credited by member firms with improving communication within the semiconductor industry, shifting the culture of firms toward long-term partnerships with equipment suppliers, and helping to establish common standards for software and manufacturing equipment. The trend toward the formation of interfirm partnerships with equipment suppliers, documented in the previous chapter, was orchestrated in large part by Sematech's Partnering for Total Quality program. Close relations between equipment suppliers and semiconductor producers have been shown to make an important contribution to the efforts of U.S. firms to improve manufacturing performance and accelerate the time-to-market for new product and process technologies.

In the crucial area of lithography, the results of Sematech's efforts have been mixed. Silicon Valley Group has emerged as a competitive manufacturer of leading-edge equipment. IBM is currently evaluating the second generation of Silicon Valley Group's Micrascan lithography system for use in 64M DRAM production (IBM took receipt of the first Micrascan II system in mid-1992). Motorola and Intel have announced that they will evaluate U.S. manufactured steppers for their leading-edge manufacturing facilities. Although it is unclear whether Silicon Valley Group will capture substantial market share, Sematech can take credit for restoring domestic capability in advanced lithography equipment. Sematech's support for GCA had less positive results. Despite showing significant improvement in product development in the late 1980s, GCA failed to return to profitability. In early 1993, GCA suspended manufacturing operations and was put up for sale by its parent company, General Signal. Several months later, Silicon Valley Group announced that it was entering into a ten-year technology-development partnership agreement with the Japanese firm Canon, one of its major competitors (Pollack 1993). The two firms will share the cost of developing next-generation equipment and divide up market areas, with Canon selling in Asia, and Silicon Valley Group in the United States.[2] The efforts of Sematech not withstanding, Silicon Valley Group needed the support of a Japanese partner to sustain necessary investment in next-generation lithography systems.

In addition to supporting equipment suppliers, Sematech has pursued a broader agenda of R&D funding that includes semiconductor manufacturing technology and procedures. Of particular significance in this regard are programs to develop computer-integrated manufacturing and flexible manufacturing systems in semiconductors, including process control software and automated materials handling capability. While initial progress has been slow, Sematech is in a good position to define

---

[2]This international agreement is similar to those negotiated by semiconductor device manufacturers: market area and customer linkages are the complementary assets that prevent partner firms from competing directly with one another.

industry-wide standards for equipment and software interface, thereby reducing the costs of developing the semiconductor "factory of the future." In addition, Sematech is conducting a series of projects involving the use of advanced simulation technologies that will likely result in further reductions in technology-development cycles.

The government has for the most part been a silent partner in Sematech. While DARPA and the GAO provide oversight, and representatives of various government agencies sit on Sematech's governing board, the agenda and activities of the organization are largely member driven. This organizational approach has helped to keep Sematech grounded in the detailed manufacturing experience of semiconductor firms, and avoids the oft-touted problem of the government being an arbiter of technological pathways. Not all semiconductor firms, however, agree with the manufacturing strategy pursued by Sematech. Of particular concern has been Sematech's shift from the development of a complete submicron fabrication process to so-called short-loop testing of manufacturing equipment (i.e., testing the performance and reliability of specific pieces of equipment). The full-line process would be of greatest benefit to small and medium-size firms that need to upgrade their manufacturing capability to submicron levels. Sematech's membership, however, is dominated by large semiconductor firms that generally already possess considerable in-house wafer fabrication and R&D capacity. Short-loop testing is of considerable utility to the latter firms because it complements their in-house R&D activities; it is of less utility to small producers.[3] In addition, notably absent from Sematech's membership are smaller start-up firms and design houses. Several of these firms have argued that their needs would be better served by a focus on new circuit design, testing, and simulation technology rather than the current emphasis on fabrication equipment.

Sematech has gone some way in addressing the immediate challenge of achieving parity with international competitors in submicron process technology and equipment. In early 1993 the consortium announced that it had achieved its goal of

[3]Several small and mid-size semiconductor firms interviewed for this study characterized Sematech as a subsidy for large producers.

establishing a 0.35 micron process line. Nevertheless, the underlying structural problem of underinvestment by private semiconductor firms in manufacturing equipment and process technology remains. For the domestic semiconductor industry to remain competitive, it must sustain high levels of investment over the long term. While the competitive position of domestic equipment manufacturers has improved, they have not yet regained substantial market share and the associated revenues necessary to fund new rounds of large-scale R&D. Moreover, there is little evidence to suggest that semiconductor firms are willing to redirect substantial amounts of their internal R&D away from product design and into equipment and process development. Rather, a substantial "free rider" problem has emerged regarding Sematech's effort to improve manufacturing equipment. Much of the benefit of a healthy domestic equipment base is available to all semiconductor firms, whether or not they are members of Sematech.[4] Sematech has been unsuccessful in recruiting new members, and two of the original members (LSI Logic and Micron Technology) left the consortium in 1992. Both of these firms indicated that, given the R&D direction taken by Sematech, their R&D funds could be more effectively used in-house. When questioned by the General Accounting Office (1992), ten of the twelve remaining members of Sematech indicated that they were unwilling to increase their funding for the consortium.

When the federal government began supporting Sematech in 1987, it was anticipated that funding would continue for a five-year period. In 1992 DARPA announced its plan to cut back support for semiconductor manufacturing to $80 million. In addition, instead of providing funds in a lump sum to Sematech, the agency suggested that it would issue R&D contracts directly to a wider range of organizations, including private firms and universities. In making this announcement, DARPA indicated that it wished to focus its activities on its stated mission of developing advanced technologies for defense

---

[4]Equipment and materials suppliers receiving support from Sematech may sell the resultant products to all semiconductor firms, whether members or nonmembers of Sematech, or domestic or foreign. The only constraint on such sales is that Sematech member firms have the right to place the first orders for new equipment.

applications. Given the strong congressional support for Sematech, it is unlikely that funding for the consortium will actually be cut in the near term. The U.S. government must now consider, however, the desirability of a longer-term commitment to Sematech and, more generally, to the domestic semiconductor industry. Contrary to the expectations of skeptical observers, Sematech has shown that it can make a difference. The question remains whether the U.S. government is willing to continue to provide targeted R&D support to the semiconductor industry, support that is not received by a multitude of other potentially worthy industries.

TRADE AGREEMENTS

The second major intervention by the U.S. government in support of the semiconductor industry has come in the area of trade relations. Of primary concern is the Semiconductor Trade Agreement signed by Japan and the United States in 1986, and subsequently revised in 1991. With this agreement, the U.S. semiconductor industry went from a system of government "manipulated" trade to one of government "managed" trade, with the focus on price floors and market-share goals (Tyson 1992). The impact of the Trade Agreement on the U.S. semiconductor industry has been mixed, marked by incremental improvements in market access rather than a fundamental change in the trading relationship between the United States and Japan (for other assessments of the agreement, see Flamm 1991; Mowery and Rosenberg 1989b; and Tyson 1992).

The 1986 Trade Agreement

The 1986 Trade Agreement was a response to a widespread perception, promoted by the Semiconductor Industry Association, of "unfair" competition from Japan. Two principal complaints were voiced. First, Japan was accused of collusive behavior in restricting sales of semiconductors by U.S. firms to Japan. In mid-1986, U.S. firms held only 8% of the Japanese semiconductor market, as compared to more than 75% of the

U.S. market for semiconductors. U.S. firms suggested that their poor sales record in Japan reflected a series of structural obstacles to fair trade, including pressure applied by the Japanese government on major Japanese electronics firms to buy semiconductors from domestic rather than foreign producers. Second, Japanese semiconductor firms were accused in the mid-1980s of "dumping" DRAMs and other semiconductors on the U.S. market at below production costs in an apparent attempt to capture market share and force U.S. firms from the market. In 1985 the U.S. International Trade Commission initiated an investigation of imports of 64K and 256K DRAM devices from Japan. The results of the investigation were announced in June 1986. The ITC found substantial evidence of sales of DRAMs at below Fair Market Value, and it instructed U.S. Customs agents to impose tariffs on Japanese imports equal to the weighted average margin of dumping (the margin ranged from 11.9% to 35.3%). In a second finding, the Commission reported evidence of dumping of Erasable Programmable Read Only Memory (EPROMs), and it recommended even higher penalties on Japanese shipments of these products.

The basis for the dumping decision has been the subject of some controversy. Dick (1991) and others have argued that the low prices charged by Japanese semiconductor firms were consistent with a goal of maximizing profits over the full product cycle of each generation of DRAM devices. In any event, the imposition of tariff penalties was avoided with the signing of a semiconductor trade agreement by the United States and Japan in August 1986. The agreement had two main elements. First, the Japanese government agreed to facilitate increased sales by U.S. firms in Japan. In a side letter to the main agreement, the full text of which has never been made public, Japan agreed to work toward a 20% U.S. share of the Japanese market by 1992. Second, on the issue of dumping, Japan agreed to provide the U.S. government with the cost information necessary to calculate price floors for DRAMs and allied memory products. Japanese semiconductor firms agreed not to sell products at prices below these values. In 1987 U.S. firms accused Japan of violating the agreement by selling DRAMs at below fair value in so-called third markets (primarily Taiwan and other Southeast

Asian countries). The United States responded by imposing punitive duties on $300 million of Japanese exports to the United States.

How successful was the 1986 Trade Agreement in meeting its goals? Two parts of the agreement can be usefully distinguished, that concerned with access to Japanese markets, and that which addressed "dumping" by Japanese semiconductor firms. Figure 6.1 shows the share of the Japanese market held by foreign semiconductor firms during the period 1986–92. Market share is calculated on the basis of the formula used by U.S. firms (i.e., excluding production by U.S. captive firms). U.S. semiconductor firms increased their share of the Japanese market from 8.6% when the agreement was signed, to 14.3% in the third quarter of 1991. During this same period, Japanese imports of integrated circuits from the United States increased by more than $1 billion. Interestingly, much of the increase in market share came as a result of higher levels of foreign purchases made by the major Japanese semiconductor firms themselves (NEC, Hitachi, and Toshiba). From the Japanese perspective, this represents a substantial movement toward the long-term objectives of the agreement. U.S. producers are less positive; they contend that incremental improvements in mar-

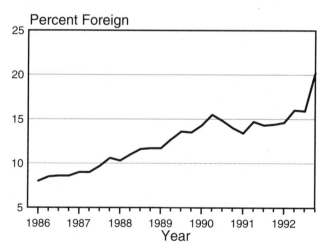

FIGURE 6.1. Foreign share of the Japanese semiconductor market, 1986–92. (Adapted from the Semiconductor Industry Association.)

ket share do not meet the desired goal of a structural change in trading relations toward a model of equal access to foreign markets.

The "dumping" provisions of the 1986 semiconductor agreement secured their immediate goal of forcing Japanese firms to raise prices on DRAMs and other products. Once low-price sales in third-country markets were curtailed in late 1987, the average selling prices on Japanese DRAM devices increased substantially and remained high throughout 1988 and 1989. Unfortunately, the consequences of this change were largely negative for U.S. firms. By the time prices began to rise, all of the major U.S. manufacturers (with the exception of Texas Instruments and Micron Technology) had already withdrawn from DRAM production. Rather than benefiting U.S. firms, therefore, the high prices created windfall profits for Japanese producers. By one estimate, inflated prices on DRAMs provided more than $5 billion in additional revenue to Japanese firms (Flamm 1991). Much of this revenue was subsequently deployed to support an expanded program of R&D and capital investment that further undermined the competitive position of U.S. firms. As previously shown in Figure 3.2, capital expenditures by Japanese semiconductor firms far exceeded those of U.S. producers during the late 1980s.

As Flamm (1991) and Tyson (1992) have indicated, one of the intermediating variables underlying the windfall profits secured by Japanese firms has been a resurgence of the role of MITI as a coordinator of manufacturing activity in the Japanese semiconductor industry. Prices on DRAMs remained high in part because of reductions in output by Japanese semiconductor firms. MITI played a key role in facilitating these cutbacks by closely monitoring demand and production conditions in DRAM markets (as it was required to do under the terms of the Trade Agreement). The revival of MITI is one of the unintended consequences of the U.S. movement toward a system of managed trade. During the mid-1970s U.S. firms protested against the activist role of MITI, which was evident in its imposition of tariff restrictions and R&D support for Japanese semiconductor firms. The success of Japanese firms during the 1980s seemed to obviate the need for such aggressive intervention. And yet the policies adopted under the semiconductor agreement have required that MITI once again assume an active role. As Flamm (1991, p. 28) suggests, U.S. policy seems caught in a contradictory position, at one time asking for less involvement by MITI, and on another occasion asking for more:

> The U.S. semiconductor industry cannot have it both ways. If American chip makers genuinely want the U.S. government to insist that MITI's postwar role as the administrative guide for Japanese industry has no place in the market-driven high-tech trading system of the 1990s, and continue to push for structural change within Japan, they cannot at the same time promote an agenda that implicitly strengthens the system of informal, behind the scenes, quasi-legal guidance they have condemned.

The 1991 Revisions to the Trade Agreement

In the summer of 1991, U.S. and Japanese government officials entered a new round of negotiations on semiconductor trade. The U.S. government was under mounting pressure from domestic producers to take a more aggressive stance in trade negotiations. The gradual improvement gained by U.S. firms in their share of the Japanese market suggested two things. First, when threatened with retaliatory tariffs, Japanese manufacturers took steps to increase marginally imports of U.S. semiconductors. Second, however, there was little evidence of a fundamental restructuring of industrial practice among Japanese electronics firms, the majority of which continued to source semiconductors primarily from domestic suppliers.

In August 1991 a second five-year agreement was signed by U.S. and Japanese representatives. In essence the new agreement endorsed the existing target of a 20% market share for U.S. producers by the end of 1992. While the 20% was moved into the main text of the agreement, it remained (despite U.S. protests) a target rather than a firm commitment by Japan. According to the text of the agreement:

> The Government of Japan recognizes that the U.S. semiconductor industry expects that the foreign market share will grow to

more than 20 percent of the Japanese market by the end of 1992 and considers that this can be realized. The Government of Japan welcomes the realization of this expectation. The two governments agree that the above statements constitute neither a guarantee, a ceiling nor a floor on the foreign market share.

In addition to changes linked to market share, and much to the relief of U.S. computer firms, the 1991 agreement abandoned the flawed policy of price floors. Japanese firms are still required to collect production cost information, which is to be provided to the U.S. government on the occasion of future dumping charges. With price floors removed, the price of DRAMs fell substantially during 1991–92, driven down in large part by emergent South Korean producers.

At the time of the signing the second agreement, U.S. firms held 14.3% of the Japanese semiconductor market (see Figure 6.1). In order to meet the 20% goal, Japanese manufacturers would have to increase substantially and rapidly their purchases of U.S.-made semiconductors. In the summer of 1992, Japan announced a series of "emergency measures" designed to ensure accelerated purchases of U.S.-made semiconductors during the second half of 1992. Among the steps taken was the preparation by the ten largest Japanese semiconductor users of lists of products that they were willing to purchase from foreign suppliers. In addition, the Japanese government sought to facilitate "design-in" agreements between Japanese firms and U.S. semiconductor producers. U.S. market share increased to 15.9% in the third quarter of 1992, and then jumped by more than 4 percentage points to 20.2% at the end of 1992. Analysis of the increase indicates that it resulted from a modest rise in the purchase of foreign semiconductors and from a shrinkage in the total market for semiconductors in Japan; in other words, the large increase was in part a reflection of recessionary conditions in Japan. As a result of this last gasp effort, Japan was able to claim that it had met the terms of the trade agreement and to avert any further movement toward trade sanctions.

The recent increases in the U.S. share of the Japanese market notwithstanding, the achievements of the semiconductor trade policy of the United States have to date been limited. The 20% target represented a relatively modest market share. Even though this immediate goal has been met, there is little evidence of a structural change in trading relations. In the absence of substantial increases in the U.S. share of the Japanese semiconductor market, additional aggressive intervention by the U.S. government seems increasingly likely. Of the variety of possible policy options, the "cautious activism" advocated by Tyson (1992, p. 132) is gaining increased support in the United States:

> If U.S. trade negotiators are not convinced that the Japanese have honored the commitment, some kind of sanction is warranted, both as a prod to further Japanese efforts and as a signal that the United States remains committed to its longstanding market access goal.

CONCLUSION

Since the mid 1980s, the U.S. government has provided substantial targeted support to the domestic semiconductor industry, both directly in the form of more than $500 million of R&D investment in Sematech, and indirectly through trade negotiations with Japan. As a result of this intervention, demonstrable (if limited) progress has been made in two key areas, namely, a strengthening of the domestic equipment-supplier base, and an incremental improvement in market access to Japan.

To what extent is government intervention in the semiconductor industry likely to be a model for other U.S. industries? First, with respect to market share, it seems likely that the overall philosophy of cautious activism advocated by Krugman (1990b), Tyson (1992), and others will become increasingly influential even if the precise policy instrument of market share goals is abandoned. Japanese trade negotiators have strongly resisted market share goals as a measure of trade performance; they seek to shift attention to less tangible indicators of the trading relationship, such as the strength of partnerships between U.S. and Japanese firms. Second, with respect to

Sematech, there is now widespread interest in the development of collaborative research consortia in other U.S. industries, from electric cars to high-definition television.

To the extent that analysts look to the semiconductor industry as a model for government intervention, it is useful to identify the operational characteristics of Sematech that have contributed to its success. In general, the research agenda of the consortium arose not from government but from the needs of the member firms. In addition, government support for Sematech, while considerable, remains only a small proportion of total R&D funding (private and public) for the semiconductor industry, thereby reducing the possibility that the consortium will lead to an overcentralization of the technology agenda.

The key to Sematech's success, however, lies in the fact that its goal has been relatively clear. U.S. firms needed to catch up in the area of manufacturing equipment and supplier relations; the parallel to the success of MITI during the late 1970s is striking. As Sematech now looks toward advancing technological capability, the number of possible technological pathways will multiply, and the possibility of backing the wrong strategy will increase. In this regard, it is interesting that the semiconductor industry is currently promoting a technology road map for the future. Labelled Micro Tech 2000, the road map has as its primary goal the manufacture of a 1 Gigabit SRAM chip, based on 0.1 micron technologies, by the year 2000. While in part an attempt at consensus building by semiconductor firms, the road map will also be used to convince Congress that there are now generally accepted technology objectives for the industry, thus providing a rationale for continued support for Sematech.

As Foray (1993) has recently indicated, the balance between experimentation and standardization in technology development—between multiple versus single technological pathways—is a crucial policy concern. Standardization and commitment to particular technological architectures certainly brings advantages of efficiency, such as reduced uncertainty and the possibility of coordinating multiple interconnecting technologies. The National Advisory Committee on Semiconductors suggests that adherence to the Micro Tech 2000 road map will allow a significant acceleration in the technology-development cycle for U.S. semiconductor firms (NACS 1992). At the same time, however, the vision of a clear path ahead remains a dangerous one; the histories of the semiconductor and other high-technology industries are replete with examples of breakthroughs that undermined existing technology trajectories.

The questions of how and when government should intervene are becoming more, not less, complex. The transition from a Cold War economy, the growing interdependence of trade and technology policy, and the emergence of intellectual property rights and commercial standards as issues of central importance to the competitive success of high-technology firms have led many to suggest that the United States now needs a coordinated approach to science and technology, one possibly managed by a civilian counterpart to DARPA. Perhaps the most significant policy challenge is the increasing globalization of high-technology manufacturing systems. In an era in which technological knowledge flows rapidly around the world, it has become increasingly difficult for the U.S. government to target its support of technology in ways that primarily benefit U.S.-based firms and workers. Technology "leakage" occurs in multiple ways—through international alliances between domestic and foreign firms, through offshore production by U.S. firms, and through the proliferation of foreign R&D laboratories in the United States. The latter serve as important listening posts for gathering and transferring knowledge and information from one country to another.

As Reich (1991) has perceptively indicated, the crucial task is that of figuring out the work of nations within the global economy. Policies that attempt to support *only* U.S.-owned firms may not be the best strategy for improving the economic welfare of U.S. residents. In the face of an increasing globalization of markets and production, there is no guarantee that firms based in the United States will keep the majority of high-wage jobs in the country. At the same time, investments by foreign-owned high-technology firms generate substantial numbers of jobs in the United States. Japanese firms, for example, currently operate more than 125 advanced technology

R&D laboratories in the United States (in the electronics, biotechnology, pharmaceutical, and other industries). The key issue for Reich (1991) and for many other policymakers is the ability of the United States to capture a large number of high-wage jobs in growing industries, regardless of whether the employer is a U.S.-owned or a foreign-owned firm.

In this regard, one of the key problems is the absence of an effective institutional structure within which to manage high-technology manufacturing in a global economy. In the vocabulary of the French regulationists (Aglietta 1979), the transition to a global mode of accumulation has gone forward ahead of the development of an adequate mode of social and institutional regulation. Rather than trying to exclude Japanese firms from access to government sponsored basic research, for example, it will likely be more advantageous for the United States to negotiate reciprocal access to research sponsored by MITI in Japan and by the JESSI consortium in Europe. Similarly, instead of the bilateral negotiations enshrined in the U.S.–Japan Semiconductor Trade Agreement, balanced trade and sustained growth will require a multilateral framework covering the multiple issues of market access, property right protection, and industrial policy. In the absence of such a multilateral agreement, trade tensions are likely to multiply and spread to additional countries, as evidenced by dumping charges recently brought against South Korean semiconductor manufacturers.

CHAPTER 7

Sources of
Competitive Advantage

Throughout the past decade, academics and policy makers have engaged in healthy debate concerning the foundations of durable-competitive advantage in semiconductors and other high-technology industries. Would the U.S. semiconductor industry follow the path of televisions, ceding manufacturing and market dominance to foreign competitors? How could U.S. firms reverse the loss of market share experienced during the first half of the 1980s? Even as the debate was taking place, U.S. semiconductor firms, in conjunction with their customers and suppliers, were moving rapidly to enhance the competitiveness of the United States in world markets. In this final chapter, I draw together the major dimensions of change in manufacturing practice and examine the implications of these changes in the U.S. semiconductor industry for other sectors of production.

MANUFACTURING SYSTEMS IN THE
SEMICONDUCTOR INDUSTRY

For much of the middle part of the twentieth century, the United States maintained a position of technological and market dominance in the semiconductor and other high-technology industries. To a significant degree, this market leadership derived from the massive buildup of the science and technology infrastructure of the United States that was initiated during the Second World War and sustained thereafter through several decades of Cold War politics. U.S. high-technology firms directly and indirectly benefited from this buildup through diverse technology investments, including federal expenditures on R&D, the expansion of private and public R&D laboratories, the training of scientists and engineers, and the important market-pull effect of defense and space procurement. For much of the postwar era, R&D investments in the United States were larger than those in all other member-nations of the Organization for Economic Cooperation and Development (OECD) combined (Mowery and Rosenberg 1990).

Beyond the sheer scale of its science and technology complex, the United States also benefited from an institutional structure of innovation that has proven remarkably effective in developing and deploying new technologies. During the past decade, researchers have documented many of the characteristics of this innovation system, including the key roles of the government as a source of funding for basic research, of universities as venues for training skilled labor, and of the start-up firm as a mechanism for rapidly exploiting the commercial and market possibilities of new technologies. Although the results of this national innovation system are evident in many fields—from the space program to supersonic aircraft—it is the semiconductor industry that best reflects both the pace of technological change and the diverse impacts of new technologies on a changing global economy.

Beginning in the late 1950s there emerged within the U.S. semiconductor industry a dynamic of rapid product and process innovation that was unusual even by the standards of high-technology sectors of production. To some extent, the model of technological development in the semiconductor industry was similar to that of other U.S. manufacturing industries, from chemicals to pharmaceuticals, and aircraft to communications equipment. Of particular note is the key role of Bell Laboratories as a source of much of the basic and applied research that underlay the initial development of semiconductor technologies. Much of the success of U.S. semiconductor firms, however, derived from their ability to create a highly original institutional structure for technology development. This structure was centered, above all, on the dense cluster of specialized semiconductor producers in Silicon Valley.

Technological innovation in the semiconductor industry was based not only on innovation in organization but also on innovation in manufacturing form. The elements of the industry's technologically dynamic manufacturing system were described in detail in Chapter 2. Perhaps the most distinctive feature of Silicon Valley has been the key role played by start-up firms as agents of technology development and change. From Fairchild Semiconductor in the 1960s, to Intel and VLSI Technology in more recent decades, start-up firms have been responsible for many important technological breakthroughs in semiconductors. The activities of start-ups have been supported by the emergence of specialized sources of venture capital (Florida and Kenney 1988) and by a local infrastructure of subcontractors and suppliers (Scott and Angel 1987).

Much of the success of start-up firms, however, derives from a broader feature of semiconductor manufacturing in Silicon Valley, namely, the rapid circulation of knowledge, ideas, and information within the region. Knowledge of new technological and market opportunities, of sources of success as well as of failure, diffuses rapidly among local firms through the mechanism of interfirm worker mobility as well as by informal contacts among workers employed by different firms. A constant flow of technological knowledge serves as a key link between large firms and start-up producers in Silicon Valley. In addition, this local exchange of information joins semiconductor producers with customers and suppliers, many of which are located within the region. Although technological dynamism rests in part on the innovative capabilities of individual firms, semiconductor manufacturers in Silicon Valley also realize substantial external economies in technology development that are central to the innovative dynamism of the production complex.

If U.S. semiconductor firms showed institutional and organizational innovation in the area of technology development, their approach to production borrowed heavily from the model of mass production that is dominant in the automobile and other older industries. The key manufacturing imperative recognized by semiconductor producers was that of reducing unit cost. U.S. semiconductor firms for the most part adopted a classic, bifurcated manufacturing form, with one segment oriented toward innovation and new product-development, the other focused on reducing the production costs of existing products. Drawing on hegemonic Fordist manufacturing principles, two key strategies emerged. The first involved achieving product-specific economies of scale through high-volume production of standard products on dedicated production lines. The second involved an attempt to reduce labor costs by relocating assembly and other routinized activities to selected low-cost sites on the global semiperiphery, especially Southeast Asia (Henderson 1989; Scott and Angel 1988). In retrospect, what is remarkable is how closely the resultant pattern of production in the semiconductor industry matched the organizational and geographical division of labor in such established industries as textiles and automobiles. The one element of the Fordist manufacturing form that semiconductor firms rejected was the acceptance of union-based employment relations. With the exception of large established firms, such as AT&T and G.E., semiconductor producers were drawn to supplies of nonunion labor outside of the established industrial centers of the Manufacturing Belt. In Silicon Valley, new immigrants and ethnic minorities were the primary source of production workers (Siegel and Borock 1982; Snow 1983).

The rigidities of mass-production systems were already in the 1960s beginning to create difficulties in established industries (Abernathy 1978); the rapid pace of technological change in the semiconductor industry dramatically intensified these problems. In emergent, technologically dynamic industries such as semiconductors, the commitment to standardized production, and the organizational separation of production and innovation as distinct stages of the manufacturing process, generated persistent problems of low production yields and fluctuating levels of capacity utilization. The tendency toward rapid technological change forced semiconductor manufacturers to continually retool their facilities at great cost; semiconductor firms experienced severe problems in matching available production capability to demand. Production yields of less than 20% were not uncommon on new product technologies. To varying degrees, these problems were experienced by all U.S. semiconductor firms.

The dominance of U.S. firms in product and process technology through the mid-1970s created a remarkable interlude during which problems of production went largely untreated. Indeed, poor yields were widely ascribed to the pace of technological change, and to the high level of miniaturization of semiconductor products, rather than to the character of the manufacturing form adopted by the industry. So long as U.S. firms retained a technological advantage over international rivals, poor manufacturing performance primarily influenced rates of profit rather than global market share. As the capability to manufacture leading-edge semiconductors diffused within the global economy, however, problems of production emerged as the key window of opportunity through which foreign competitors could capture market share from U.S. firms. The challenge came first from Japan, and occurred at the point of greatest weakness, namely, the poor production yields achieved by U.S. semiconductor firms. Using product technology licensed from U.S. firms, and manufacturing equipment initially purchased from U.S. equipment suppliers, Japanese manufacturers demonstrated the possibility of achieving high yields on leading-edge production lines, thereby confounding the received wisdom concerning the limits on manufacturing performance under conditions of rapid technological change.

From the late 1970s onward, Japanese firms were able to capture a substantial share of the world market for semiconductor devices. By the mid-1980s, Japan had surpassed the United States as the largest producer of semiconductor devices in the world. The foundations for the rapid rise of the Japanese semiconductor industry were described in detail in Chapter 3. How Japan achieved commercial success in semiconductors is an issue of considerable complexity, involving aggressive government intervention, a relatively closed market, and large-scale investments in R&D and manufacturing capacity. The key factor in Japan's rapid growth, however, has been a willingness to break with the bifurcated manufacturing form characteristic of semiconductor production in the United States. Japanese semiconductor firms achieved high yields and low product-failure rates by integrating production into the manufacturing process as a whole. A commitment to device performance and technological sophistication was balanced by a concern for the manufacturability of products and the development of product and process technologies that permitted high production yields. Japanese semiconductor firms devoted substantial re-sources to identifying sources of device failure on the produc-tion line, and to systems of production automation that im-prove manufacturing yields.

During the 1980s Japanese semiconductor firms estab-lished a dominant position in DRAMs and allied commodity integrated circuits. In addition, Japan emerged as a leader in several key areas of semiconductor process technology, includ-ing production equipment and materials. With DRAMs as the leading process driver in the semiconductor industry, most analysts believed that it was only a matter of time before Japanese firms would diversify into other product markets and come to dominate the global industry. In the event, a series of developments confounded the expectations of industry observ-ers. Of primary importance were the dramatic advances made by U.S. firms in improving production yields and in reducing time-to-market on new product and process technologies. In addition, the ongoing transformation of semiconductor tech-nology and production processes, and the rise of South Korea as a major manufacturer of DRAMs, undermined the strategy of high-volume production on which much of the Japanese semiconductor industry is based.

Chapter 4 described the strategies used by U.S. semicon-ductor firms to improve manufacturing performance. Two key analytical themes were presented. One is the increasing "Japan-ization" of U.S. manufacturing systems, involving, in particu-lar, the establishment of much closer cooperative ties among customers, semiconductor producers, and equipment suppli-ers, and the institution of multidimensional product teams as the key agents of change in production. U.S. firms have learnt from their Japanese competitors, and the result has been a convergence of the manufacturing performance of U.S.

and Japanese firms. The second theme is the increasing integration of technology development and production within U.S. semiconductor firms. This integration is supplanting a previously fragmented manufacturing form in ways that allow for a more rapid deployment of new technologies and for enhanced yields in production. In its clearest articulation, integration involves the physical combination of product development and production within so-called development facilities. The resultant geography represents a marked break with the previously dominant spatial and international divisions of labor within high-technology manufacturing systems.

With the convergence of U.S. and Japanese production performance during the 1980s, a key dimension of the manufacturing advantage of Japanese firms has been diminished. In addition, U.S. firms have reduced their time-to-market for new technologies, thereby undermining the ability of Japanese firms to diversify from DRAMs into other design-intensive product markets, such as microprocessors and high-density, application-specific devices. In turn, the failure of Japanese firms to move into new markets became a key problem during the late 1980s, when South Korean firms emerged as major producers of DRAM devices. In cutting prices to maximize market share, Korean firms have followed the strategy used earlier by Japanese firms; as of late 1992, South Korean firms had captured approximately 20% of the DRAM market, dramatically reducing the revenues and market share held by Japanese producers. This reversal of fortune for Japanese firms has called into question the basis for competitive success in the semiconductors industry, and has challenged much of the conventional wisdom concerning international competitive advantage in high-technology industries.

COMPETITIVE ADVANTAGE IN THE SEMICONDUCTOR INDUSTRY

The globalization of semiconductor manufacturing has provided a substantial challenge to existing accounts of the sources of international competitiveness in high-technology industries.

During the 1960s it was widely believed that the United States would retain its position of technological and market leadership in semiconductors. As outlined in Chapter 3, established economic development theory emphasized the cumulative and self-reinforcing character of competitive advantage in advanced technology development. By this account, the early leaders in new technologies are able to prolong their manufacturing advantage by drawing on accrued knowledge and experience. The rise to dominance of Japanese semiconductor firms during the 1980s, however, provided dramatic testimony to the fact that governments can intervene strategically to overcome existing economies and shift competitive advantage from one nation to another. More recently, the emergence of South Korea as a major supplier of DRAMs indicates that the capability to manufacture advanced technology does diffuse rapidly among advanced industrial economies.

If, as the experience of Japan and South Korea suggests, "first-mover" advantages are an insufficient barrier-to-entry for international competitors, what are the potential sources of durable competitive advantage in the semiconductor and other high-technology industries? Two competing theories have been identified. The first, widely voiced within the U.S. semiconductor industry during the mid-1980s, suggests that dominance in global semiconductor markets would rest on alternative sources of oligopolistic advantage, namely, control over process technology and high-volume markets. The basis for this argument is the historic role of DRAMs as the primary process driver in the semiconductor industry. Firms involved in the manufacture of DRAMs (i.e., Japanese semiconductor manufacturers) would be the first to develop next-generation process technologies and could leverage this advantage to dominate the market for leading-edge products. Lacking immediate access to the latest process technology, U.S. and other firms not involved in DRAM production would lose market share over time. U.S. leadership in product technology and design systems would be negated by constrained access to process technology.

This scenario carries considerable influence within the U.S. semiconductor industry. For example, it provided the rationale for the failed attempt in 1989 by seven U.S. firms raise funds for U.S. Memories, a jointly owned DRAM manufacturing operation. In addition, the National Advisory Committee on Semiconductors continues to view participation in high-volume consumer markets as the key to long-term competitive survival in the semiconductor industry (NACS 1992). Recent events suggest, however, that the anticipated problem of constrained access to leading-edge technology is overstated. First, a number of alternative process drivers have emerged, including Static Random Access Memories (SRAMs) and other memory devices. Moreover, the process gap that previously existed between DRAMs and logic devices has substantially narrowed, as shown, for example, by LSI Logic's announcement of a 0.65 process for Application-Specific Integrated Circuits (ASIC) devices. Second, the ability to manufacture semiconductors based on advanced submicron process technology is spreading to other advanced industrial nations, suggesting that Japan or any other nation will have great difficulty exerting oligopolistic control over the technology. The scenario is made all the more unlikely by the proliferation of international alliances for the development of advanced process-technology. With R&D costs for the next generation of process technology likely to exceed $1 billion, Japanese producers have initiated technology development agreements with U.S., European, and South Korean firms; these alliances will inevitably serve to diffuse further technological capability among participating firms. Third, while DRAM production plays a key role in advancing lithography and certain other dimensions of the fabrication process, advances in design technologies and flexible manufacturing are more closely associated with microprocessors, ASICs, and other design-intensive products. In short, leadership in manufacturing DRAMs and allied commodity circuits is not a sufficient basis for maintaining technology and market dominance in semiconductors.

A contrasting theoretical perspective rejects any attempt to ground profitability in a static advantage, such as control over DRAMs or any other market or technology. Rather, firms must compete over the long term by establishing dynamic advantage

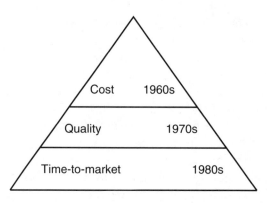

FIGURE 7.1. Production imperatives in the U.S. semiconductor industry.

in the form of an ability continually to develop markets, products, and production capability ahead of other firms. To a significant degree, U.S. semiconductor firms are now restructuring their manufacturing operations to meet this goal. Figure 7.1 illustrates how the production imperatives of the U.S. semiconductor industry have changed during the past three decades.[1] During the 1960s, the production operations of U.S. firms were organized primarily to achieve lower production costs. As indicated above, this involved both the exploitation of product-specific economies of scale, and the search for cheap labor and other low-cost factor input. During the 1970s, issues of production quality (i.e., production yields and product reliability) were *added* to the charge of minimizing production costs. U.S. semiconductor operations were restructured to match international standards of production performance (e.g., through the implementation of quality improvement programs). Finally, during the 1980s, time-to-market emerged as an added key concern. Much of the current restructuring of manufacturing practice and production form in the U.S. semiconductor industry is directed toward the goal of reducing the development time for new products without sacrificing quality or production cost.

[1] I am grateful to Dr. Dennis Buss, vice president of technology development at Analog Devices, for suggesting this schematic.

FUTURE PROSPECTS

A dramatic turnaround in the market fortunes of the U.S. semiconductor industry is underway. Although detailed market information is not yet available, most industry analysts now agree that U.S. firms have, for the first time since 1985, captured the largest share of the worldwide semiconductor market. VLSI Research, a semiconductor consulting firm, estimates that in 1992 U.S.-based firms were responsible for 43.8% of worldwide merchant semiconductor shipments, as compared to a 43.1% market share held by Japanese firms. By contrast, in 1990 Japanese producers held close to 50% of the worldwide merchant semiconductor market. Many U.S. firms, such as Intel and Texas Instruments, have recorded substantial increases in both revenues and profits that are to a significant degree the result of an accelerated pace of development of new technology. The increase in market share is further confirmation of the improved competitiveness of U.S. semiconductor firms in world markets.

The rapid shift in market share must be treated with some caution, however, for it derives as much from weaknesses in the Japanese economy as from refound strength in U.S. semiconductor manufacturing. Two points need to be emphasized in this regard. First, the slowdown in the Japanese economy, and especially the recessionary conditions in the automobile and consumer electronics industries, is a key factor in the loss of market share by Japanese semiconductor firms. Japanese firms continue to buy most of their semiconductors from domestic suppliers. On this account, the slowdown in the Japanese economy disproportionately impacts domestic semiconductor suppliers. By the same token, when the Japanese economy emerges from recession, it is likely that Japanese semiconductor firms will regain much of the market share they lost in 1992. Second, of greater long-term concern to Japan is the loss of revenue from, and global market share in, DRAMs. It is estimated that Hyundai, Samsung, and other South Korean firms have captured approximately 20% of the worldwide DRAM market, with virtually all of this gain occurring at the expense of Japanese firms. Moreover, competition from South Korea has forced the price of DRAMs to new lows, further undermining the revenue stream of Japanese semiconductor firms.[2]

In addition to improvements in U.S. manufacturing performance, an indication of the increasing competitiveness of U.S. semiconductor producers is the way they have responded to the most recent period of recession. Historically, U.S. firms have done well during periods of economic slowdown, only to lose substantial market share during periods of rapid growth. This pattern reflects in large part the tendency of Japanese semiconductor manufacturers to maintain high levels of investment throughout the boom and bust cycles of demand for semiconductors. When demand for semiconductors grew rapidly, it was Japanese semiconductor manufacturers that had the leading-edge production capacity to meet the demand. During the past two years, however, Japanese semiconductor firms cut back on capital investment (by more than 10% in 1992), while many U.S. producers added to existing fabrication capacity. Among the U.S. firms that have announced new or expanded fabrication facilities are Advanced Micro Devices, Intel, Motorola, and Texas Instruments. Plant and equipment expenditures by Intel in 1992 exceeded $1 billion, an investment far larger that that of any other semiconductor manufacturer in the world. The availability of additional leading-edge fabrication capacity will help to ensure large-volume production of the next-generation microprocessors and other design-intensive products that U.S. firms will introduce in early 1993.

The most likely scenario for the U.S. semiconductor industry in the 1990s is that its market share will stabilize at or close to the current level. However, two critical steps must be taken in order to maintain market share. First, U.S. semiconductor firms must continue to improve manufacturing performance and accelerate development of new technology. Japanese and other foreign competitors are currently making large R&D investments in factory automation, advanced man-

---

[2]In 1992 Micron Technology filed a dumping petition with the U.S. International Trade Commission against South Korean DRAM manufacturers. Much to the relief of U.S. computer firms, the final ruling imposed only minor tariff penalties, ranging from 0.74% to 7.19%, that are likely to have little impact on DRAM prices.

ufacturing equipment, and flexible manufacturing technologies. While the competitive prospects of the U.S. equipment industry have improved, new rounds of investment in manufacturing technology are required. As indicated in Chapter 6, the U.S. has yet to resolve the underlying structural problem of underinvestment in manufacturing technology and equipment. In the near term, continued government support will be required, either in the form of extended funding for Sematech, or through a broader initiative, such as R&D investment tax credits. Second, the issue of trade relations will grow in importance in the 1990s as more electronics production and assembly occurs outside of the United States. Of particular concern here is the continued rapid expansion of the Asian market for semiconductors. In order to retain their current share of world semiconductor shipments, U.S.-based firms must *increase* their share of semiconductor shipments to Japan and other foreign markets.

LEARN FROM JAPAN, AND LOSE?

U.S. semiconductor firms learned much from their Japanese competitors during the 1980s. From quality improvement program to incremental innovation and close partnerships with customers and suppliers, the "Japanization" of U.S. manufacturing practice has been an important element of the restructuring process in the U.S. semiconductor industry. Moreover, in providing targeted support for Sematech, the U.S. government relied heavily on the model of MITI in Japan. As this convergence in manufacturing practice takes place, the challenge facing U.S. semiconductor firms, and U.S. high-technology industries in general, is how to retain the best aspects of the existing innovation system. Of greatest concern is the possibility that, in creating structures to sustain a process of continuous innovation, U.S. industry will undermine its ability to achieve breakthrough innovations (such as its development of the planar process around which semiconductor fabrication is based, and of the microprocessor). Breakthrough innovations define the trajectory of technological development and

offer the opportunity for an "end run" around existing manufacturing advantage.

Two emergent trends in United States are of concern in
this regard. First, there are some signs that the United States is
cutting back its commitment to basic research. The percentage
of gross national product devoted to R&D is now lower in the
United States than in Japan and in the former West Germany
(National Science Board 1991). During the past five years, R&D
expenditure in the United States grew at a constant dollar rate
of only 1.2%. Several of the major industrial R&D laboratories
in the United States have reoriented their efforts from basic to
applied research. More generally, high-technology firms are
under continuing pressure to shorten their investment time-
horizons and bolster short-term profitability, putting at risk
their long-term technological capability.

Second, the forms of entrepreneurial industrialization that
contributed much to the innovative dynamism of the U.S. semiconductor industry are currently being threatened by a severe
shortage of investment capital. Critics of chronic entrepreneur-
ship (e.g., Ferguson 1988) will likely shed no tears over this
trend. The present analysis suggests, however, that U.S. interests would be better served by a restructuring of the process
of new firm formation than by a dearth of start-up firms. In
recent years, the major criticism of start-up firms has revolved
around the accelerated transfer of technology to foreign competitors, typically through licensing agreements with offshore
foundries. Start-up firms are driven into these licensing agreements by a shortage of investment capital, and in particular by
the difficulty of obtaining financing for production facilities.
These impediments can be overcome by increasing the number
of production facilities that are jointly owned by several U.S.-
based firms. Partnerships and joint ventures will continue to
proliferate in the semiconductor industry during the coming
decade.

In practice, the concepts of incremental and breakthrough
innovation simply represent the end points of a continuum; the
majority of technological and organizational innovations occur
somewhere in the middle (Gordon 1992). To a significant degree, competitive success in semiconductors now depends upon

a dynamic of continuous innovation, one that involves advances, both large and small, in technology, markets, and production processes. Throughout this book, I have argued that the principal barrier to achieving the goal of continuous innovation is the organizational and geographical separation of innovation and production within U.S. semiconductor manufacturing systems. Since the mid-1980s, U.S. semiconductor firms have taken dramatic steps to overcome this fragmented manufacturing form, seeking to reintegrate production into the technology-development process. While the long-term effects of these efforts are far from clear, changes in manufacturing practice and industrial structure have already had an important impact on the competitiveness of U.S. semiconductor firms. Manufacturing performance has improved, and market share has stabilized. The changes implemented by U.S. semiconductor firms, in conjunction with equipment suppliers and with the support of Sematech and other government programs, constitute nothing less than a remaking of the U.S. semiconductor industry.

Survey Methodology and Sample

The research presented in Chapters 4 and 5 is based on the results of a questionnaire survey of U.S. semiconductor firms that was administered in August and September 1991. The purpose of the survey was to determine the ways in which U.S. semiconductor firms had responded to the changed conditions of intensified international competition during the second half of the 1980s. The questionnaire survey covered numerous dimensions of manufacturing practice, including relations with external customers and suppliers, participation in cooperative technology-development agreements, and the overall organization and geography of the manufacturing process. The questionnaire survey was supplemented by lengthy follow-up interviews with senior management and engineering staff at forty of the participating semiconductor firms, including all of the largest merchant and captive producers. These interviews provided further insight into the character of the restructuring process that is under way in the industry.

The questionnaire survey was directed to U.S. manufacturers of integrated circuits, including both design houses that subcontract out the actual fabrication of semiconductor products, and merchant and captive firms that operate their own production facilities. In order to enhance the consistency of the survey sample, the analysis excluded several small groups of specialized semiconductor firms: (a) manufacturers of so-called chipsets (e.g., Chips and Technology, and Multichip Technology); (b) firms that exclusively manufacture gallium arsenide devices (e.g., Gazelle and Vitesse Semiconductor); and (c) captive firms whose involvement in the semiconductor industry is limited to R&D (e.g., Cray Computer). Firms that only manufacture simple discrete or hybrid semiconductor devices were also excluded from the study.

The questionnaire was mailed to 122 U.S. manufacturers of integrated circuits. Standard survey follow-up procedures were used to maximize the response rate to the questionnaire. Of the 122 firms, 72 agreed to participate in the study and returned completed questionnaires, yielding a response rate of 59.0%. Of the 72 participating firms, 24 (33.3%) were design houses that subcontract out all wafer fabrication, and 48 (66.7%) were firms that operate one or more wafer fabrication facilities. By way of comparison, 49 (33.8%) of the 145 U.S.-based integrated circuit manufacturing firms are design houses. Of the 72 sample firms, 11 (15.3%) were large producers with annual sales of integrated circuits of more than $200 million in 1990; the remaining firms were smaller producers with specialized product lines. In short, the survey sample contained a wide variety of firms located in Silicon Valley and elsewhere in the United States that manufacture integrated circuits.

Semiconductor firms participating in the study were promised confidentiality, and the results of the survey are reported in the form of group averages only. Information presented in the book on individual firms was obtained during follow-up interviews and appears with the consent of the individuals and firms involved. Additional data were obtained from government documents and other published sources.

References

Abernathy, W. 1978. *The Productivity Dilemma*. Baltimore: Johns Hopkins University Press.

Aglietta, M. 1979. *A Theory of Capitalist Regulation*. London: New Left Books.

Amin, A., and Robins, K. 1990. The re-emergence of regional economies? The mythical geography of flexible accumulation. *Environment and Planning D; Society and Space* 8: 7–34.

Angel, D. 1989. The labor market for engineers in the U.S. semiconductor industry. *Economic Geography* 65: 99–112.

Angel, D. 1990. New firm formation in the semiconductor industry: Elements of a flexible manufacturing system. *Regional Studies* 24: 211–221.

Angel, D. 1991. High technology agglomeration and the labor market. *Environment and Planning A* 23: 1501–1516.

Angel, D. In press. Tighter bonds? Customer–supplier linkages in semiconductors. *Regional Studies*.

Arrow, K. J. 1962. Economic welfare and the allocation of resources for invention. In National Bureau Committee for Economic Research (Ed.), *The Rate and Direction of Inventive Activity*. Princeton: Princeton University Press.

Asher, N., and Strom, L. 1977. *The Role of the Department of Defense in the Development of Integrated Circuits*. Arlington, VA: Institute for Defense Analysis.

Aydalot, P., and Keeble, D. 1988. *High Technology Industry and Innovative Environments: The European Experience*. New York: Routledge, Chapman and Hall.

Borrus, M. 1988a. Chipwars: Can the U.S. regain its advantage in microelectronics? *California Management Review* 30: 64–79.

Borrus, M. 1988b. *Competing for Control*. New York: Ballinger.

Borris, M., Millstein, J., and Zysman, J. 1982. *International Competition in Advanced Industrial Sectors*: *Trade and Development in the Semiconductor Industry*. Washington: Government Printing Office.

Braun, E., and MacDonald, S. 1982. *Revolution in Miniature*. Cambridge, England: Cambridge University Press.

Camagni, R. (Ed.). 1991. *Innovation Networks*. London: Belhaven Press.

Clark, P., and Staunton, N. 1989. *Innovation in Technology and Organization*. New York: Routledge.

Cohen, W., and Levin, R. C. 1989. Empirical studies of innovation and market structure. In R. Schmalensee and R. Willig (Ed.), *Handbook of Industrial Organization* (pp. 1059–1107). Amsterdam: North Holland.

Contractor, F., and Lorange B. (Eds.). 1988. *Collaborative Strategies in International Business*. Lexington, MA: Lexington Books.

Dick, A. R. 1991. Learning by doing and dumping in the semiconductor industry. *Journal of Law and Economics* 34:133–159.

Dixit, A., and Norman, V. 1980. *Theory of International Trade*. Cambridge: Cambridge University Press.

Dosi, G. 1982. Technological paradigms and technological trajectories. *Research Policy* 11: 147–162.

Dosi, G. 1984. *Technical Change and Industrial Transformation: The Theory and an Application to the Semiconductor Industry*. London: Macmillan.

Dosi, G., Freeman, C., Nelson, R., Silverberg, G., and Soete, L. (Eds.). 1988. *Technical Change and Economic Theory*. London: Pinter.

Dosi, G. 1990. *The Economics of Technical Change and Trade*. New York: Wheatsheaf.

Drucker, P. 1990. The emerging theory of manufacturing. *Harvard Business Review* 90: 94–102.

Eisenhardt, K., and Schoonhoven, C. 1990. Organizational growth: Linking founding team, strategy, environment, and growth among U.S. semiconductor ventures, 1978–88. *Administrative Science Quarterly* 35: 504–529.

Ernst, D. 1983. *The Global Race in Microelectronics*. New York: Campus Verlag.

Ernst, D., and O'Connor, D. 1992. *Competing in the Electronics Industry: The Experience of Newly Industrializing Economies*. London: Pinter.

Ferguson, C. 1988. From the people who brought you voodoo economics. *Harvard Business Review* 88: 55–62.

Flamm, K. 1991. Making new rules. *Brookings Review* 9: 22–28.

Florida, R., and Kenney, M. 1988. Venture capital, high technology, and regional development. *Regional Studies* 22: 33–48.

Florida, R., and Kenney, M. 1989. High technology industrialization in the USA and Japan. *Environment and Planning A* 22: 233–257.

Florida, R., and Kenney, M. 1990a. *The Breakthrough Illusion*. New York: Basic Books.

Florida, M., and Kenney, M. 1990b. Silicon Valley and Route 128 won't save us. *California Management Review*, 33: 68–88.

Florida, R., and Kenney, M. 1992. *Beyond Mass Production*. New York: Basic Books.

Foray, D. 1993. General introduction. In D. Foray and C. Freeman (Eds.), *Technology and the Wealth of Nations* (pp. 1–24). London: OECD.

Foray, D., and Freeman, C. (Eds.). 1993. *Technology and the Wealth of Nations*. London: OECD.

Fortune. 1959. *Fortune Product Directory*. Trenton: Fortune Directories.

Freeman, C. 1987. *Technology Policy and Economic Performance*. London: Pinter.

Freeman, C. 1992. Networks of innovators: A synthesis of research issues. *Research Policy* 20: 1–42.

Gertler, M. 1988. The limits to flexibility: Comments on the post-Fordist vision of production and its geography. *Transactions of the Institute of British Geographers* 13: 419–432.

Gertler, M. 1992. Flexibility revisited: Districts, nation states and the forces of production. *Transactions of the Institute of British Geographers* 17: 259–278.

Glasmeier, A. 1985. Innovative manufacturing industries: Spatial incidence. In M. Castells (Ed.), *High Technology, Space and Society* (pp. 55–79). Beverly Hills, CA: Sage.

Glasmeier, A. 1988. Factors governing the development of high technology agglomerations: A tale of three cities. *Regional Studies* 22: 287–301.

Glasmeier, A. 1991. *The High-Tech Potential*. New Brunswick, NJ: Rutgers University Press.

Gomory, R. 1989. From the ladder of science to the product development cycle. *Harvard Business Review* 89: 99–106.

Gordon, R. 1992. *Inter-Firm Networks and Innovation in Silicon Valley*. Paper presented at the annual meeting of the Association of American Geographers, San Diego CA.

Gupta, A., and Wileman, D. 1990. Accelerating the development of new products. *California Management Review* 32: 24–44.

Hakansson, H. (Ed.). 1987. *Industrial Technological Development: A Network Approach*. London: Croom Helm.

Harrington, J. W. 1985. Intra-industry structural change and locational change: U.S. semiconductor manufacturing, 1958–80. *Regional Studies* 19: 343–352.

Haslam, C. 1987. The end of mass production? *Economy and Society* 16: 405–439.

Henderson, J. 1989. *The Globalisation of High Technology Production*. London: Routledge.

Hirst, P., and Zeitlin, J. 1991. Flexible specialization versus post-Fordism: Theory, evidence and policy. *Economy and Society* 20: 1–55.

Hoefler, D. 1968, July 8. Semiconductor family tree. *Electronic News*, p. 1.

Holmes, J. 1986. The organization and locational structure of production subcontracting. In A. J. Scott and M. Storper (Eds.), *Production, Work, Territory: The Geographical Anatomy of Industrial Capitalism* (pp. 80–106). Boston: Allen and Unwin.

Integrated Circuit Engineering Corporation. 1992. *Status 1992*. Scottsdale, AZ: ICE.

Japan's semiconductor equipment makers challenge U.S. lead. 1990, February. *Tokyo Business Today* 16–17.

Johnson, C. 1985. *MITI and the Japanese Miracle*. Stanford: Stanford University Press.

Johnson, C., Tyson, L., and Zysman, J. (Eds.). 1989. *Politics and Productivity*. Cambridge, MA: Ballinger.

Jorde, T., and Teece, D. 1990. Innovation and cooperation: Implications for competition and anti-trust. *Journal of Economic Perspectives* 4: 75–96.

Kendrick, J. 1992. Quality of U.S.-made semiconductors for military integrated circuits is improving. *Quality* 31: 11.

Kogut, B., and Kim, D. 1991. *Strategic Alliances of Semiconductor Firms*. Unpublished report to Dataquest.

Krugman, P. 1979. Increasing returns, monopolistic competition, and international trade. *Journal of International Economics* 9: 469–479.

Krugman, P. (Ed.). 1986. *Strategic Trade Policy and the New International Economics*. Cambridge, MA: MIT Press.

Krugman, P. 1990a. *Rethinking International Trade*. Cambridge, MA: MIT Press.

Krugman, P. 1990b. Does the new trade theory require a new trade policy? *World Economy* 4: 423–442.

Krugman, P. 1991. *Geography and Trade*. Cambridge, MA: MIT Press.

Landau, R., and Rosenberg, N. 1986. *The Positive Sum Strategy: Harnessing Technology for Economic Growth*. Washington, DC: National Academy Press.

Langlois, R. 1992. *Capabilities and Vertical Disintegration in Process Technology: The Case of Semiconductor Fabrication Equipment.* Consortium on Competitiveness and Cooperation, Working Paper 92-10. Berkeley: University of California.

Levin, R. 1982. Innovation in the semiconductor industry. In H. Fusfeld and R. Langlois (Eds.), *Understanding R&D Productivity* (pp. 37–54). Elmsford, NY: Pergamon Press.

Link, A., and Bauer, L. 1989. *Cooperative Research in U.S. Manufacturing.* Lexington, MA: Lexington Books.

Lovering, J. 1991. Theorizing post-Fordism: Why contingency matters. *International Journal of Urban and Regional Research* 15: 298–301.

Malecki, E. 1983. Technology and regional development: A survey. *International Regional Science Review* 8: 89–125.

Malecki, E. 1991. *Technology and Economic Development.* Harlow, England: Longman.

Malerba, K. 1985. *The Semiconductor Business.* London: Francis Pinter.

Markusen, A., Hall, P., Campbell, C., and Deitrick, S. 1991. *The Rise of the Gunbelt: The Remapping of Industrial America.* London and Boston: Allen and Unwin.

Morgan, K., and Sayer, A. 1988. *Microcircuits of Capital.* Cambridge, MA: Polity Press.

Morris, P. 1990. *A History of the World Semiconductor Industry.* London: Peregrinus.

Mowery, D. 1988. *International Collaborative Ventures in U.S. Manufacturing.* Cambridge, MA: Ballinger.

Mowery, D., and Rosenberg, N. 1989a. *Technology and the Pursuit of Economic Growth.* Cambridge, MA: Cambridge University Press.

Mowery, D., and Rosenberg, N. 1989b. New developments in U.S. technology policy: Implications of competitiveness and international trade policy. *California Management Review* 32: 107–124.

Mowery, D., and Rosenberg, N. 1990. *The U.S. National Innovation System.* Consortium on Competitiveness and Cooperation, Working Paper 90-3. Berkeley: University of California.

Mytelka, L. 1990. *Strategic Partnerships: States, Firms and International Competition.* London: Pinter.

National Advisory Committee on Semiconductors. 1989. *A Strategic Industry at Risk.* Washington, DC: Author.

National Advisory Committee on Semiconductors. 1992. *Attaining Preeminence in Semiconductors.* Washington, DC: Author.

National Research Council. 1992. *U.S.-Japan Strategic Alliances in the Semiconductor Industry.* Washington, DC: National Academy Press.

National Science Board. 1991. *Science and Engineering Indicators.* Washington, DC: Government Printing Office.

Nelson, R. 1959. The simple economics of basic scientific research. *Journal of Political Economy* 67: 297–306.

Nelson, R., and Wright, G. 1992. The rise and fall of American technological leadership: The post-war era in perspective. *Journal of Economic Literature* 30: 1931–1964.

Oakey, R. 1981. *High Technology Industry and Industrial Location.* Aldershot: Gower.

Okimoto, D., Sugano, T., and Weinstein, F. 1984. *Competitive Edge: The Semiconductor Industry in the United States and Japan.* Stanford: Stanford University Press.

Ostry, S. 1990. *Governments and Corporations in a Shrinking World.* New York: Council on Foreign Relations.

Parkhe, A. 1993. "Messy" research, methodological predispositions, and theory development in international joint ventures. *Academy of Management Review* 18: 227–68.

Perez, C. 1985. Microelectronics, long waves and world structural change: New perspectives for developing countries. *World Development* 3: 441–463.

Piore, M. 1992. Technological trajectories and the classical revival in economics. In M. Storper and A. Scott (Eds.), *Pathways to Industrialization and Regional Development* (pp. 156–170). London: Routledge.

Piore, M., and Sabel, C. 1984. *The Second Industrial Divide.* New York: Basic Books.

Pollack, A. 1993, June 6. After a long fight, U.S. yields on a vital chip making tool. *New York Times,* p. F4.

Pollert, A. 1988. Dismantling flexibility. *Capital and Class* 34: 42–75.

Porter, M. 1990. *The Competitive Advantage of Nations.* New York: Free Press.

Prestowitz, C. 1988. *Trading Places.* New York: Basic Books.

President's Council on Competitiveness. 1992. *The Legacy of Regulatory Reform.* Washington, DC: U.S. Government Printing Office.

Rauch, J. 1993. The realities of our times: The Semiconductor Chip Protection Act of 1984 and the evolution of the semiconductor industry. *Journal of Patent and Trademark Office* 75: 93–124.

Reich, R. 1991. *The Work of Nations.* New York: Knopf.

Reich, R., and Mankin, E. 1986. Joint ventures with Japan give away our future. *Harvard Business Review* 86: 78–85.

Rice, V. 1987a, February. CMOS acceptance spans complementary markets. *Electronic Business,* p. I.

Rice, V. 1987b, August. The upstart startups, *Electronic Business*, pp. 46–64.

Rogers, E., and Larsen, J. 1984. *Silicon Valley Fever*. New York: Basic Books.

Rosenberg, N. 1982. *Inside the Black Box*. Cambridge, England: Cambridge University Press.

Sabel, C. 1989. Flexible specialization and the re-emergence of regional economies. In P. Hirst and J. Zeitlin (Eds.), *Reversing Industrial Decline* (pp. 17–70). Oxford, England: Berg.

Saxenian, A. 1983. The urban contradictions of Silicon Valley. *International Journal of Urban and Regional Research* 17: 237–261.

Saxenian, A. 1990. Regional networks and the resurgence of Silicon Valley. *California Management Review* 33: 89–112.

Saxenian, A. 1991. *The Origin and Dynamics of Production Networks in Silicon Valley*. Institute of Urban and Regional Development, Working Paper. Berkeley: University of California.

Sayer, A. 1990. Post-Fordism in question. *International Journal of Urban and Regional Research* 13: 666–695.

Schoenberger, E. 1989. Thinking about flexibility: A response to Gertler. *Transactions of the Institute of British Geographers* 14: 98–108.

Schoonhoven, C., Eisenhardt, K., and Lyman, K. 1990. Speeding products to market: Waiting time to first product introduction in new firms. *Administrative Science Quarterly* 35: 177–207.

Schumpeter, J. 1934. *The Theory of Economic Development*. New York: Oxford University Press.

Schumpeter, J. 1954. *Capitalism, Socialism and Democracy*. London: Unwin University Books.

Scott, A. 1988a. Flexible production systems and regional development: The rise of new industrial spaces in North America and Western Europe. *International Journal of Urban and Regional Research* 12: 171–185.

Scott, A. 1988b. *New Industrial Spaces*. London: Pion.

Scott, A., and Angel, D. 1987. The U.S. semiconductor industry: A locational analysis. *Environment and Planning A* 19: 875–912.

Scott, A., and Angel, D. 1988. The global assembly operations of U.S. semiconductor firms: A geographical analysis. *Environment and Planning A* 20: 1047–1067.

Scott, A., and Storper, M. 1990. *Regional Development Reconsidered*. Lewis Center for Regional Policy Studies, Working Paper 1. Los Angeles: University of California.

Semi/Sematech. 1992. *America is Back: 1991–92 Status Report*. Austin, TX: Author.

Siegel, L., and Borock, H. 1982. *Background Report on Silicon Valley*:

Report to the U.S. Commission on Civil Rights. Mountain View, CA: Pacific Studies Center.

Snow, R. 1983. The new international division of labor and the U.S. workforce: The case of the electronics industry. In J. Nash and M. Fernandez Kelly (Eds.), *Women, Men, and the International Division of Labor* (pp. 39–69). Albany, NY: SUNY Press.

Steinmueller, W. 1992. The economics of flexible integrated circuit manufacturing technology. *Review of Industrial Organization* 7: 327–349.

Stewart, C. 1967. Wage structures in an expanding labor market: The electronics industry in San Jose. *Industrial and Labor Relations Review* 21: 73–91.

Storper, M. 1992. The limits to globalization: Technology districts and international trade. *Economic Geography* 68: 60–93.

Storper, M., and Christopherson, S. 1987. Flexible specialization and regional industrial agglomeration: The case of the U.S. motion picture industry. *Annals of the Association of American Geographers* 77: 104–117.

Storper, M., and Walker, R. 1989. *The Capitalist Imperative.* New York: Basil Blackwell.

Stowsky, J. 1989. Weak links, strong bonds. In C. Johnson, L. Tyson, J. Zysman (Eds.), *Politics and Productivity,* (pp. 241–274.). Cambridge, MA: Ballinger.

Teece, D. 1986. Profiting from technological innovation: Implications for integration, collaboration, licensing, and public policy. *Research Policy* 15: 286–305.

Teece, D. 1990. *Innovation and the Organization of Industry.* Consortium on Competitiveness and Cooperation, Working Paper 90-6. Berkeley: University of California.

Tilton, J. 1971. *International Diffusion of Technology.* Washington, DC: Brookings Institution.

Tyson, L. A. 1992. *Who's Bashing Whom? Trade Conflict in High Technology Industries.* Washington, DC: Institute for International Economics.

United Nations Center on Transnational Corporations. 1986. *Transnational Corporations in the International Semiconductor Industry.* New York: Author.

U.S. Congress, Committee on Governmental Affairs. 1989. *Prospects for the Development of a U.S. HDTV Industry.* Washington, DC: U.S. Government Printing Office.

U.S. Congress, Committee on Science, Space, and Technology. 1990. *Federal Research Policy and the American Semiconductor Industry.* Washington, DC: U.S. Government Printing Office.

U.S. Congress, Congressional Budget Office. 1987. *The Benefits and Risks of Federal Funding for Sematech.* Washington, DC: U.S. Government Printing Office.

U.S. Congress, Congressional Budget Office. 1990. *Using R&D Consortia for Commercial Innovation: Sematech, X-Ray Lithography and High Resolution Systems.* Washington, DC: U.S. Government Printing Office.

U.S. Congress, Office of Technology Assessment. 1990. *The Big Picture: HDTV and High-Resolution Systems.* Washington, DC: U.S. Government Printing Office.

U.S. Department of Commerce. 1979. *A Report on the U.S. Semiconductor Industry.* Washington, DC: U.S. Government Printing Office.

U.S. Department of Commerce. 1988. *JTECH Panel Report on Computer Integrated Manufacturing and Computer Assisted Design for the Semiconductor Industry.* McLean, VA: SAIC.

U.S. Department of Commerce, Bureau of the Census. 1958–82. *Census of Manufactures.* Washington, DC: U.S. Government Printing Office.

U.S. Department of Commerce, Bureau of the Census. 1964–89. *County Business Patterns.* Washington, DC: U.S. Government Printing Office.

U.S. Department of Defense. 1987. *Defense Semiconductor Dependency.* Washington, DC: U.S. Defense Science Board.

U.S. General Accounting Office. 1990. *Federal Research: Sematech's Efforts to Strengthen the U.S. Semiconductor Industry.* Washington, DC: Author.

U.S. General Accounting Office. 1991. *Federal Research: Sematech's Efforts to Develop and Transfer Manufacturing Technology.* Washington, DC: Author.

U.S. General Accounting Office. 1992. *Federal Research: Sematech's Technological Progress and Proposed R&D Program.* Washington, DC: Author.

U.S. International Trade Commision. 1986. *64K Dynamic Random Access Components from Japan.* USITC Publication 1862. Washington, DC: Author.

Westney, D. E. 1991. *Country Patterns in R&D Organization: The United States and Japan.* Center for International Studies, Working Paper 91-06. Cambridge, MA: MIT Press.

Williamson, O. 1985. *The Economic Institutions of Capitalism: Firms, Markets and Relational Contracting.* New York: Free Press.

Wilson, R., Ashton, P., and Egan, T. 1980. *Innovation, Competition, and Government Policy in the Semiconductor Industry.* Lexington, MA: Lexington Books.

Index